An Interactive Discovery-Based Language Arts U

Grades 6-8

Fables & Folktales

Darcy O. Blauvelt & Richard G. Cote

PRUFROCK PRESS INC.
WACO, TEXAS

Prufrock Press Inc.
P.O. Box 8813
Waco, TX 76714-8813
Phone: (800) 998-2208
Fax: (800) 240-0333
http://www.prufrock.com

Fables & Folktales

Table of Contents

Lessons

Introduction

Background

Gifted program directors, resource specialists, and—perhaps most importantly—general education classroom teachers who struggle with the challenge of providing appropriate services to students of high potential in the traditional classroom may be interested in these Interactive Discovery-Based Units for High-Ability Learners. The units encourage students to use nontraditional methods to demonstrate learning.

Any given curriculum is composed of two distinct, though not separate, entities: content and context. In every classroom environment, there are forces at work that define the content to be taught. These forces may take the form of high-stakes tests or local standards. But in these Interactive Discovery-Based Units for High-Ability Learners, the context of a traditional classroom is reconfigured so that students are provided with a platform from which to demonstrate academic performance and understanding that are not shown through traditional paper-and-pencil methods. This way, teachers go home smiling and students go home tired at the end of the school day.

C = C + C
Curriculum = Content + Context

In March of 2005, the Further Steps Forward Project (FSFP) was established and funded under the Jacob K. Javits Gifted and Talented Students Education Program legislation. The project had a two-fold, long-range mission:

- The first goal was to identify, develop, and test identification instruments specific to special populations of the gifted, focusing on the economically disadvantaged.
- The second goal was to create, deliver, and promote professional development focused on minority and underserved populations of the gifted, especially the economically disadvantaged.

The result was the Student Context Rubric (SCR), which is included in each of the series' eight units. The SCR, discussed in further depth in the Appendix, is a rubric that a teacher or specialist uses to evaluate a student in five areas: engagement, creativity, synthesis, interpersonal ability, and verbal communication. When used in conjunction with the units in this series, the SCR provides specialists with an excellent tool for identifying students of masked potential—students who are gifted but are not usually recognized—and it gives general education teachers the language necessary to advocate for these students when making recommendations for gifted and additional services. The SCR also provides any teacher with a tool for monitoring and better understanding student behaviors.

Using best practices from the field of gifted education as a backdrop, we viewed students through the lens of the following core beliefs as we developed each unit:

- instrumentation must be flexible in order to recognize a variety of potentials;
- curricula must exist that benefit all students while also making clear which students would benefit from additional services; and
- identification processes and services provided by gifted programming must be integral to the existing curriculum; general education teachers cannot view interventions and advocacy as optional.

These eight contextually grounded units, two in each of the four core content areas (language arts, social studies, math, and science), were developed to serve as platforms from which middle school students could strut their stuff, displaying their knowledge and learning in practical, fun contexts. Two of the units (*Ecopolis* and *What's Your Opinion?*) were awarded the prestigious National Association for Gifted Children (NAGC) Curriculum Award in 2009, and two others (*Order in the Court* and *Mathematics in the Marketplace*) were awarded Curriculum Awards in 2011. Over the span of 3 years, we—and other general education teachers—taught all of the units multiple times to measure their effectiveness as educational vehicles and to facilitate dynamic professional development experiences.

The FSFP documented that in 11 of 12 cases piloted in the 2008–2009 school year, middle school students showed statistically significant academic gains. In particular, those students who were underperforming in the classroom showed great progress. Furthermore, there were statistically significant improvements in students' perceptions of their classroom environments in terms of innovation and involvement. Finally, the contextually grounded units in this series can be used as springboards for further study and projects, offering teachers opportunities for cross-disciplinary collaboration.

Administrators, teachers, and gifted specialists will gain from this series a better sense of how to develop and use contextualized units—not only in the regular education classroom, but also in gifted programming.

How to Use the Units

Every lesson in the units includes an introductory section listing the concepts covered, suggested materials, grade-level expectations, and student objectives. This section also explains how the lesson is introduced, how students demonstrate recognition of the concepts, how they apply their knowledge, and how they solve related problems. The lesson plans provided, while thorough, also allow for differentiation and adaptation. Depending on how much introduction and review of the material students need, you may find that some lessons take more or less time than described. We have used these units in 50-minute class periods, but the subparts of the lesson—introducing the material, recognizing the concepts, applying knowledge, and solving a problem—allow for adaptability in terms of scheduling. The "Additional Notes" for each lesson provide further tips, flag potential problem areas, and offer suggestions for extending the lesson.

This series offers many contextual units from which to choose; however, we do not recommend using them exclusively. In our research, we have found that students who are constantly involved in contextual learning become immune to its benefits. We recommend, therefore, that you vary the delivery style of material across the school year. For most classes, spacing out three contextual units over the course of the year produces optimal results.

These units may be used in place of other curriculum. However, if you find that your students are stumbling over a specific skill as they progress through a unit, do not hesitate to take a day off from the unit and instead use direct instruction to teach that skill. This will help to ensure that students are successful as they move forward. It is necessary for students to be frustrated and challenged, as this frustration serves as the impetus of learning—yet they must not be so frustrated that they give up. Throughout the unit, you must find the delicate balance between providing challenges for your students and overwhelming them.

The Role of the Teacher

A contextual unit is a useful vehicle both for engaging your students and for assessing their abilities. As a teacher, your role changes in a contextual unit. Rather than being the driving force, you are the behind-the-scenes producer. The students are the drivers of this creative vehicle. If you are used to direct instruction methods of teaching, you will need to make a conscious choice not to run the show. Although this may feel a bit uncomfortable for you in the beginning, the rewards for your students will prove well worth the effort. As you become more comfortable with the process, you will find that this teaching method is conducive to heightening student engagement and learning while also allowing you to step back and observe your students at work.

Group Dynamics

Cooperation plays a key role in this unit. Small-group work is fraught with challenges for all of us. Creating groups that will be able to accomplish their objectives—groups whose members will fulfill their roles—takes some forethought. Keep in mind that sometimes the very act of working through any issues that arise may be the most powerful learning tool of all. Before beginning the unit, you should discuss with students the importance of working together and assigning tasks to ensure that work is distributed and completed fairly and equally.

Preparation and Pacing

Deciding on a timeline is very important as you plan the implementation of the unit. You know your students better than anyone else does. Some students may be more successful when they are immersed in the unit, running it every day for 3 weeks. Others would benefit from having some days off to get the most out of their experiences.

Every classroom is different. Students possess different sets of prior knowledge, learning strategies, and patterns. This means that as the teacher, you must make decisions about how much of the material you will introduce prior to the unit, whether you will provide occasional traditional instruction throughout the unit, how many days off you will give students, and how much your students will discover on their own throughout the course of the unit. For example, in this language arts unit, students learn about the various elements of a story (beginning, middle, end, theme, character, and so on). You might easily incorporate this unit into your existing language arts lesson plans, in order to give students a more nuanced understanding of what they are reading. Alternatively, you might allow students to work with books that they select for themselves, analyzing them through the lens of what they learn in this unit. There are many opportunities to extend the learning and differentiate the contents of this book, and it will be up to you to determine how you mold the resources we have provided here in order to best fit your classroom and students.

Also, you should feel free to use materials other than those suggested. If there is a topic or source that is highly relevant for your students, then it might be worthwhile for you to compile research sites, articles, and other materials about the topic in order to provide your students a degree of real-world involvement.

Using these units is a bit like using a recipe in the kitchen. The first time you use one of the units, you may want to use it just as it is written. Each successive time you use it, however, you may choose to adjust the ratios and substitute ingredients to suit your own tastes. The more you personalize the units to your students' situations and preferences, the more engaged they will be—and the same goes for you as the teacher.

Grade-Level Expectations

All of our units are aligned with New Hampshire's Grade-Level Expectations. These state requirements are similar to many states' GLEs, and we hope that they will be useful for you. For each lesson, we have listed the applicable New Hampshire GLEs in a format that illustrates which learning objectives students are meeting by completing the given tasks.

Adaptability

"Organized chaos" is a phrase often used to describe a contextual classroom. The students are not sitting at their desks and quietly taking notes while the teacher delivers information verbally. A classroom full of students actively engaged in their learning and creatively solving real-world problems is messy, but highly productive. Every teacher has his or her own level of tolerance for this type of chaos, and you may find yourself needing days off occasionally. Organization is an essential ingredient for success in a contextual unit. For example, you will need a place in your classroom where students can access paperwork. It is important to think through timeframes and allow for regular debriefing sessions.

You will also want to develop a personalized method for keeping track of who is doing what. Some students will be engaged from the start, but others you will need to prod and encourage to become involved. This will be especially true if your students are unfamiliar with this type of contextual learning. There are always a few students who try to become invisible so that classmates will do their work for them. Others may be Tom Sawyers, demonstrating their interpersonal skills by persuading peers to complete their work. You will want to keep tabs on both of these types of students so that you can maximize individual student learning. Some teachers have students keep journals, others use daily exit card strategies, and others use checklists. Again, many aspects of how to use these units are up to you.

It is difficult in a busy classroom to collect detailed behavioral data about your students, but one advantage of contextual learning is that it is much easier to spend observation time in the classroom when you are not directly running the show! If you have the luxury of having an assistant or classroom visitor who can help you collect anecdotal data, then we recommend keeping some sort of log of student behavior. What has worked well for us has been to create a list of students' pictures, with a blank box next to each picture in which behaviors can be recorded.

Contextual units require the teacher to do a considerable amount of work prior to beginning the unit, but once you have put everything into place, the students take over and you can step back and observe as they work, solve problems, and learn.

Unit Overview

This unit focuses on making students more aware of written and performed storytelling conventions. It aims to engage students in storytelling, to encourage students to feel more comfortable and confident as storytellers, to guide students in providing self-reflection and peer feedback, and to help students better understand the conventions, terms, and methods associated with written and oral stories.

The unit was designed to be used in conjunction with an authentic performance assessment entitled *Folktales* developed by Dr. Tonya Moon, Dr. Carolyn Callahan, Dr. Catherine Brighton, and Dr. Carol A. Tomlinson under the auspices of the National Research Center on the Gifted and Talented. The unit is divided into three sections: skill building, writing workshops, and performance.

Skill building provides a framework to ensure that students have the basic skills necessary to enable them to complete the lessons and ultimately the authentic performance assessment project, a storytelling festival. These skills include experience and knowledge of various folktales, writing skills such as word choice and story structure (beginning, middle, and end), and the elements of public speaking.

The writing workshop section of the unit begins by introducing students to the task of developing their own stories to tell in the storytelling festival. This portion of the unit allows the students time in class to work on the development of their stories, keeping in mind the guidelines put forth by the rubric. As students are workshopping their own and each other's stories, they will use the skills they have learned, and they will offer constructive feedback to their peers. During this portion, teachers can have one-on-one time with students who may need more individual guidance as the storytelling festival nears.

The performance aspect of the unit is a storytelling festival. This can be structured to fit your students' abilities, your time constraints, your classroom situation, and so on. It can take place in a single day or over the course of several class periods, it can be held in various locations, and many other modifications can be made depending on your class's needs and resources.

Each lesson is structured to include the elements of introduction, recognition, application, and problem solving. As the teacher, you introduce the concept of the lesson. The students are then given the opportunity to demonstrate that they recognize the concept, and they are then provided the opportunity to apply the concept before they solve a problem using that concept. By organizing each lesson into these four divisions, we hope to offer you latitude in differentiating the lesson based on your students' prior knowledge, skills, levels of engagement, and readiness. Thus, it will fall to you to determine how to modify the lessons and where to start each student. With this unit, as with all of the units, we encourage you to familiarize yourself with the lessons and then make whatever changes you like to help your class derive the most benefits.

Unit Outline

We designed these lessons to be used during 50-minute class periods. Depending on the extent to which you need to review concepts with your students, and the amount of time you decide to devote to particular activities, some of these lessons may take fewer or more days than indicated. We have tried to note how many days each lesson will take to complete.

Lesson 1

First, the teacher discusses various parts of a story, including beginnings, middles, and ends. Students first work in groups to create stories with randomly selected parts (character, setting, and so forth), and then they use what they have learned to complete improvised stories that they share with the class. Students are introduced to the concept of constructive criticism and peer feedback, and they practice offering such feedback as their peers are sharing their stories. Students fill out a self-evaluation that gives the teacher information about their preferred learning and performing styles.

Lesson 2

Students demonstrate a working knowledge of the concepts of beginning, middle, and end by evaluating (individually) a story chosen from a class library of short books and/or picture books. Terms and concepts are reviewed and introduced, including *folktale, fairytale, fable, trickster tale,* and *how and why story.* Working in groups, students analyze stories and switch beginnings, middles, and endings with other groups to create new stories. Students start portfolios, which can be graded at the end of the unit or can simply be used to help them as they prepare for the storytelling festival later on. (*Note*: This lesson requires 2 days.)

Lesson 3

The class discusses word choice and its role in storytelling, focusing on the role of nouns, adjectives, verbs, and adverbs. Students create descriptions using both pictures and words to better understand the relationship between verbal and visual description. Students create storyboards for remembered or imagined stories to demonstrate the interplay between verbal and visual description.

Lesson 4

Students learn or review the concepts of eye contact, projection, enunciation, and tempo. Then in groups, they perform tongue twisters for the class to demonstrate an understanding of these concepts. Students practice giving and receiving constructive criticism.

Lesson 5

The teacher demonstrates and discusses the difference between telling a story and acting out a story. Students continue to practice offering constructive feedback. Students use the provided story library of familiar stories in order to develop their storytelling stills, working in small groups. (*Note*: This lesson requires 2 days.)

Lesson 6

Students receive the prompt and guidelines for the authentic performance assessment project, a storytelling festival. The teacher discusses the prompt, guidelines, and associated information with students, who begin to plan their projects using the provided worksheets to help them develop characters and plots. (*Note*: This lesson requires 2 days.)

Lesson 7

Students are introduced to the rubric that will be used to score their final storytelling presentations, and the rubrics are discussed. Students complete their planning sheets, which should be approved by the end of this lesson. The teacher assists students who are having difficulty, using the provided story cards that review types of stories and concepts.

Lesson 8

The class works on converting written work into performed work, continuing to practice giving and receiving constructive criticism. Students focus on the concepts of stressing words, using volume, incorporating sound effects, using facial expressions, and making eye contact. Students work in pairs to practice these techniques. (*Note*: This lesson requires 2 days.)

Lesson 9

Students finish and rehearse their stories in preparation for the festival. Students complete a step chart ensuring that they have covered all of the necessary concepts. This chart will be filled out by the students themselves and by their peers, giving students peer-review feedback in addition to their self-critique. (*Note*: This lesson requires 2 days.)

Lesson 10 (Storytelling Festival)

The storytelling festival takes place. There are many aspects of the storytelling festival that are up to the teacher depending on the students and the situation, including audience, location, and time. Students offer each other written feedback, and each student completes a self-evaluation after reviewing the feedback that he or she received from peers and the teacher. (*Note*: This lesson requires 2 days.)

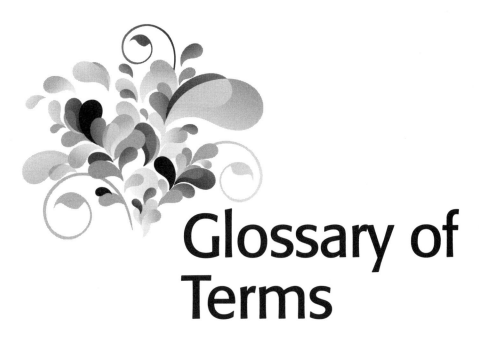

Glossary of Terms

For the purposes of this unit, the following definitions will be used.

- **Constructive Criticism:** Feedback phrased in a positive way that enables the recipient to learn from his or her mistakes and capitalize on his or her strengths.
- **Enunciation:** Speaking clearly, a skill that is essential to public performing. To pronounce a word distinctly, a speaker must form the consonants clearly. Pacing is also important in successful enunciation.
- **Fable:** A simple story that often uses animals as its central characters. Fables generally have morals, or central messages meant to be taught via the fable.
- **Fairytale:** A complex story that uses magic or enchantment as a focal point of the story.
- **Folktale:** A make-believe story that uses symbolism, dramatic language, and exaggerated characters to convey a message for all ages.
- **How and Why Story:** A story devised to explain a natural phenomenon; it is not based in scientific fact.
- **Moral/Message:** The lesson the story teaches (e.g., Goldilocks learned to listen to her parents and not go into others' houses uninvited).

- **Presentation:** How colorful images are created through pictures and words.
- **Projection:** The use of the diaphragm to support the voice in order for the speaker to be heard clearly by others. Projection should not be confused with yelling.
- **Sequencing:** The flow of the beginning, middle, and end of a story.
- **Symbolism:** Elements of a story that represent other things or concepts (e.g., the Big Bad Wolf represents evil, Rapunzel's hair represents her own resources).
- **Tempo:** The pace at which the speech is delivered; it must be fast enough to keep listeners' attention, but slow enough to be understood.
- **Theme:** The central meaning or lesson of the story.
- **Tone:** The way somebody speaks or writes that indicates what that person is feeling or thinking. Inflection and word choice play important roles in tone.
- **Trickster Tale:** A story that uses a main character who tries to deceive, swindle, or trick the other characters. Most often, the trickster loses in the end in order to teach a lesson.
- **Universal Theme:** A theme that is present in stories from many different cultures and can be understood by all audiences (e.g., love conquers evil).
- **Volume:** The level of sound produced by a speaker. This is different from projection, which describes the mechanics of making oneself heard. The volume used by a speaker can be modified in order to reflect what is happening in the story (e.g., speaking loudly when conveying a character's anger), as well as to keep the audience engaged (e.g., speaking softly to create suspense).
- **Word Usage:** The words chosen by a writer or speaker, which are important for being specific, engaging the reader, and creating a certain tone.

Lesson 1

Concepts
- Beginning (establishes the characters and setting of the story)
- Middle (introduces the problem or conflict contained in the story)
- End (resolves the problem or conflict of the story)

Materials
- Self-Assessment sheet (p. 18)
- Story cards (pp. 19–27)

Student Objective
The teacher leads a discussion about the concepts of beginnings, middles, and ends of stories. Students work in groups to formulate plots and present them based on randomly chosen elements, and then students improvise stories individually and share them with the class.

Introduction
After the students complete the self-assessment form, the teacher introduces or reviews the following concepts:
- the sequence of the story, including the beginning (the character and setting of the story are established), the middle (the problem or dilemma contained within the story is introduced and unfolds), and the end (the problem is resolved);
- the theme of the story (the lesson or moral); and
- constructive criticism (responding to pictures, stories, and performances in a positive way that will allow the author or performer to improve his or her work).

Recognition

Students write their own definitions for the three parts of a story, and they describe their own preferred communication styles (e.g., performance, writing, speaking, drawing). The teacher uses the results of this free-response preassessment, along with the sheet provided, to put the students in small groups based on their communication preferences.

Application

Students use the provided materials to conduct a group activity wherein they tell a story using a preferred mode of communication to demonstrate the concepts learned.

1. Each student picks a character card.
2. Each group picks a setting card, a problem card, and a theme card.
3. Group members work to create a story that links all of their pieces together, no matter how farfetched.
4. Each group presents its story to the class in its preferred mode of communication.
5. The class responds with constructive criticism and feedback.

Problem Solving

Students write their own stories.

1. Students concentrate on the "who" of the story (the physical description, motivation, and changes in character), the "where" of the story (the setting, including descriptions based on the five senses), the "what" of the story (the plot and the climax), and the "why" and "how" of the story (the believability of the story and how the ending links to the previous information).
2. Students share their stories with the class.
3. The class responds with constructive criticism and feedback.

Grade-Level Expectations

The student:

- Demonstrates initial understanding of elements of literary texts by identifying or describing characters, setting, problem, solution, or plot, as appropriate to text.
- Identifies significant changes in character or setting over time.

Additional Notes

- As you plan your use of this unit, it is important that you feel free to substitute words and concepts that you have already introduced to your students if we are using different words (e.g., "rising action" instead of "middle"). If you have presented differently worded definitions for beginning, middle, end, or any other terms, students will already be comfortable with these definitions.

- Giving students a choice in terms of how they present material (e.g., performing, writing, drawing) is important not only because it allows students to play to their strengths, but also because it can help shyer students to transition more naturally into speaking in front of people.

- It is helpful to copy the different cards on different-colored paper. This way, it is easy to sort them out at the end. Laminating the cards may also be useful. You might make your own cards if there are certain characters, settings, and so forth you know your class would enjoy or that relate to other topics you've been studying.

- You should have a discussion with students about what constructive criticism and feedback entail. You might model this for them and ask them to practice with you before having them provide feedback for their classmates. When students are providing feedback in this lesson, you could have them identify and discuss beginnings, middles, and ends of stories, as well as any other components or vocabulary you'd like to incorporate.

- In the Problem Solving section of this lesson, you could make several adaptations. You might have students use the cards from their groups for character, place, and so on, creating a different story than their groups did; you might have them draw new cards; you might have them draw one or two cards (e.g., for character and setting), but make up the other components; or you might have them invent all of the components of their stories. A final option would be to allow students to choose whether or not to use cards.

Name:_____ Date: _____

Self-Assessment

Please answer the following questions as honestly as possible.

1. I can speak in front of a group with expression, creating a picture with my words.

   ⬭   ⬭   ⬭   ⬭
   NEVER   **SOMETIMES**   **OFTEN**   **ALWAYS**

2. I can identify the setting, character, plot, and problem/solution in a story and how they can change as the story is told.

   ⬭   ⬭   ⬭   ⬭
   NEVER   **SOMETIMES**   **OFTEN**   **ALWAYS**

3. I can understand the different genres of storytelling such as fairytales, fables, how and why stories, and trickster tales.

   ⬭   ⬭   ⬭   ⬭
   NEVER   **SOMETIMES**   **OFTEN**   **ALWAYS**

4. I can describe a character from a story and tell you about how that character thinks, acts, and feels.

   ⬭   ⬭   ⬭   ⬭
   NEVER   **SOMETIMES**   **OFTEN**   **ALWAYS**

5. I can use what I know and my own experiences in my writing.

   ⬭   ⬭   ⬭   ⬭
   NEVER   **SOMETIMES**   **OFTEN**   **ALWAYS**

Beginning Cards: Who (Character)

Teacher	Parent
Child	Movie Star
Woods Guide	Fisher
Cook	Customer

Opera Singer	Rock Star
President	Villain
Thief	Police Officer
Dancer	Clown

Fables and Folktales © Prufrock Press Inc.
Permission is granted to photocopy or reproduce this page for single classroom use only.

Artist	Banker
Nurse	Doctor
Captain	Dog Walker
Shopper	TV Host

Beginning Cards: Where (Setting)

Farm	Library
School	Home
Woods	Movie Theater
Kitchen	Store

Fitness Club	Hospital
Beach	Large City
Cruise Ship	Airplane
School Bus	Cafeteria

Middle Cards: What (Dilemma/Problem)

You are lost.

You ran out of gas.

The electricity has gone out.

One of you has broken your leg.

Someone stole your prize pig.

You lost your homework.

You lost your cell phone.

The volcano is about to erupt.

You have a flat tire.

You cannot find your parents.

You are about to run out of food.

The water supply is drying up.

A mysterious character is stealing all of the books.

A spaceship has landed nearby.

Only one of you can be the star of the show.

You have a secret that you must tell in order to save everybody.

Ending Cards: Why (Moral/Theme)

Honesty is the best policy.	Keep your hands to yourself.
Friends are your best resources.	Be yourself.
Work hard to get ahead.	Necessity is the mother of invention.
Trust is the foundation of a friendship.	Gossip hurts people.

Creativity is a blessing, not a curse.

Be kind to strangers.

Trust your intuition.

Look both ways before crossing the street.

Always be prepared.

Tolerance of others is important.

A good night's sleep is the best medicine.

A smile a day keeps the doctor away.

Lesson 2

Concepts

- Beginning of a story
- Middle of a story
- End of a story

Materials

- Story Evaluation sheet (p. 31)
- Types of Stories sheet (p. 33)
- Classroom set of fairytales, folktales, fables, trickster tales, and how and why stories at a variety of reading levels
- Student portfolios (pocket folders)

Student Objective

Students demonstrate a working knowledge of the concepts of beginning, middle, and end by evaluating a story.

Introduction

The class reviews and discusses material.
- The class discusses various types of stories using the Types of Stories sheet.
- Using the Types of Stories sheet, the teacher defines the term *folktales* and discusses its implications using common references. The terms *fairytale*, *fable*, *trickster tale*, and *how and why story* are also introduced, along with *word usage*, *symbolism*, *presentation*, and *theme*.
- The class reviews the concepts of beginning, middle, and end, along with any other terms that may have been discussed (e.g., *conflict*).

Recognition

The teacher solicits examples of story categories, and students explain the importance of all three story parts within these categories using examples from familiar stories.

Application

Students read critically and work in groups.

1. Each student chooses a story from those available (class story bank) and reads it.
2. Students fill out the Story Evaluation sheet.
3. Students present their findings in small groups and then turn in their story evaluations to the teacher.

Problem Solving

Students work in discussion groups to dissect a story and understand its workings.

1. Each group is either assigned a story or may choose a story. (These should be short stories or picture books due to time constraints.) Each group breaks the story into its three constituent parts.
2. Each group writes a brief description of the three parts of its story on three separate sheets of paper.
3. Each group keeps the beginning of its story (retaining the same characters) and then trades the middle and ending parts with other groups, ensuring that each group has a beginning, middle, and ending from three different groups (the beginning being from the group itself).
4. Each group develops a story that weaves together the parts, and then each group acts out its story for the class.

Grade-Level Expectations

The student will:

- Demonstrate an initial understanding of elements of literary texts by identifying or describing character(s), setting, problem/solution, and plot, as appropriate to the text; and by identifying any significant changes in character or setting over time.
- Analyze and interpret elements of literary texts, citing evidence where appropriate by describing characters' traits, motivations, or interactions and citing thoughts, words, or actions that reveal characters' traits, motivations, or changes over time.
- Demonstrate an initial understanding of elements of literary texts by identifying the characteristics of a variety of types/genres of literary texts (e.g.,

poetry, plays, fairytales, fantasy, fables, realistic fiction, folktales, historical fiction, mysteries, science fiction, myths, legends).

- Analyze and interpret elements of literary texts, citing evidence where appropriate by making inferences about cause and effect, external conflicts (e.g., person versus person, person versus nature/society/fate), and the relationships among elements within text (e.g., how the historical era influences the characters' actions or thinking).

Additional Notes

- In order for students to have sufficient time to analyze their stories, the stories used for the group activity will have to be quite short. (The point of the lesson is students' evaluation of the stories, rather than the reading itself.) We have found that picture books work very well and are fun for students. Be sure to plan ahead in order to have a large enough collection of picture book versions of different types of stories. Your school librarian will be a good resource for this, but if your middle school library does not have these types of books, you or your librarian may need to request books from an elementary school library. (You could also personally check out books from your local library, if it has a better selection.)

- The problem-solving activity, wherein student groups mix and match beginnings, middles, and endings, is a fun challenge and can be done at several points during the unit if you have spare time.

- When selecting books, try to branch out from the more traditional stories and select tales from different cultures. An Internet search will yield many excellent modern folktales and fairytales that have been recast or reimagined to be more inclusive and diverse.

- The small groups used for the Application and Problem Solving sections could be the same, but you might have students switch groups.

- At this point in the unit, you should be sure that each student has a way of organizing his or her materials. We generally use simple two-pocket folders for our students to stay organized. This way, whatever you do not collect can be kept in the folders, and students can use elements of their previous work in later lessons and reflect on their progress at the end of the unit.

Name:_____ Date: _____

Story Evaluation

NAME: _____

BOOK TITLE:_____

TYPE OF STORY: _____

What makes this book the type of story you classified it as above?

_____

_____

_____

_____

_____

Complete the following outline.

BEGINNING:

_____

_____

_____

_____

_____

MIDDLE:

_____

_____

_____

_____

_____

END:

_____

_____

_____

_____

_____

THEME:

_____

_____

_____

Types of Stories

FOLKTALE

A make-believe story that uses symbolism, dramatic language, and exaggerated characters to convey a message that people of all ages can learn from.

FAIRYTALE	FABLE	TRICKSTER TALE	HOW AND WHY
A complex story that uses magic or enchantment as a focal point of the story.	A simple story that often uses animals as the central characters and that teaches an important moral lesson.	A story that uses a main character who tries to deceive, swindle, or trick the other characters. He always loses in the end.	A story devised to explain a natural phenomenon that is not based in scientific fact.
Example: Cinderella	**Example:** The Tortoise and the Hare	**Example:** Native American stories with trickster coyotes	**Example:** A story explaining why the sun rises and sets

TERMS

WORD USAGE: The words a story uses to convey mood, setting, character, and so on. Does the story use active verbs, descriptive adjectives, and a variety of nouns to tell the tale?

SYMBOLISM: Using people, animals, or things to represent ideas or themes in a story. For example, wolves often symbolize evil. Does the story contain any symbols that stand in for ideas or messages?

PRESENTATION: The way a story is told (verbally, visually, through performance). Does the story create colorful scenes through words, actions, voice, and so forth?

SEQUENCING: The order of the story. Are the beginning, middle, and end clear?

THEME: The message of the story. For example, "Struggles in life are unavoidable, but if one perseveres, that person can triumph over the odds." Is the story's message clear?

Fables and Folktales © Prufrock Press Inc.

Permission is granted to photocopy or reproduce this page for single classroom use only.

33

Lesson 3

Concepts

- Nouns
- Adjectives
- Verbs
- Adverbs

Materials

- Paper
- Markers
- Page 36 in Brian Jacques's *Seven Strange and Ghostly Tales* (or descriptive passage in another book)
- Scoring Guide sheet (p. 37)

Student Objective

Students create descriptions by using both pictures and words for nouns, adjectives, verbs, and adverbs.

Introduction

The teacher reads a passage from a book to the class, modeling performances that are expected from students when they read aloud (e.g., using expression, clear diction, and eye contact).

Recognition

Students review the parts of speech and how they are used to create descriptions. The teacher rereads the passage from the Introduction section to students, and students draw as many images as they can from the descriptive language used.

Application

Students use verbal and visual description to communicate a character or setting from their imagination or memory.

1. Students choose whether to write or illustrate a brief description of a character or a setting. Illustrations should be done on the top half of the paper, with written descriptions on the bottom half.
2. Once students have completed either the illustration or the written description, they switch with a classmate. If the first student drew an illustration, then the second student should write a description to go along with that illustration. If the first student wrote a description, then the second student should illustrate it.
3. Students should discuss how they interpreted one another's work.

Problem Solving

Students use what they have learned about the parts of a story and descriptive language to create storyboards of stories with which they are familiar.

1. Discuss your expectations of students' storyboards, and define *storyboard* for students who are unfamiliar with the term (storyboards are graphic outlines of stories, but students can have leeway in how they represent the various story elements).
2. Students' storyboards should depict beginning, middle, and end, as well as relevant characters and settings.
3. Students should choose stories with which they are familiar, so that they can create complete, fleshed-out storyboards.

Grade-Level Expectations

The student will:

- Demonstrate an initial understanding of elements of literary texts by identifying or describing character(s), setting, problem/solution, and plot, as appropriate to the text; or by identifying any significant changes in character and setting over time.
- Analyze and interpret elements of literary texts, citing evidence where appropriate, by describing characters' traits, motivations, and interactions and citing thoughts, words, or actions that reveal characters' traits, motivations, and changes over time.

Additional Notes

- We commonly use a passage from Brian Jacques's book *Seven Strange and Ghostly Tales* for the Introduction and Recognition portions of this lesson, but you can substitute a passage of your choosing. Whatever passage you choose should have a lot of descriptive language and should describe a scene with numerous components. We have included a scoring guide to evaluate students' analyses of the passage. This scoring guide corresponds to the Jacques passage, so if you choose a passage with a different number of objects to look for in students' drawings, you can modify the guide or make your own.

- You should assure students that their scores are for comparison, not for a grade. These evaluations are useful for class discussion about what people noticed most, as well as to help identify students' learning styles. It is always interesting for us to review the illustrations that students generate after having listened to the passage. Because they are listening to the passage and *then* drawing their impressions, we are able to assess not only their auditory processing skills, but also their recall.

- The Application activity, wherein students complete one another's impressions by either drawing or writing, is very engaging for kids. It is up to you whether or not to inform them that they will be completing each other's impressions—you may elect simply to tell them at first that they have the choice between written and visual description. Watching them realize that it will fall to someone else to interpret their words or pictures is very interesting! Remember to stress the tenets of constructive criticism for this exercise, particularly if students have not been informed that their descriptions will be shared and subject to interpretation. You can either collect these or have students keep them in their portfolios; if you let them keep them, be sure to specify which sheets students will keep (i.e., the text, the image, the combination they started, the combination they finished).

- When students are creating storyboards, you might consider making this a group activity, depending on the amount of time you have. Students could make more involved storyboards or use technology.

- By the end of this lesson, students should have a good grip on the concepts of beginnings, middles, and ends as well as the different types of stories. If you have students who are still struggling with these concepts, consider inserting a direct instruction day or providing individual help or activities in order to clear up any confusion.

Scoring Guide

How many items from Brian Jacques's *Seven Strange and Ghostly Tales* did the student include? The student earns a point for each item represented in his or her illustration.

Half moon	❑
Gravel path	❑
Person (Jamie)	❑
Stone angels	❑
Crosses	❑
Gravestones	❑
Gate	❑
Two other people	❑
Bushes	❑
Shadow	❑

Total: _____

Lesson 4

Concepts

- Eye contact
- Projection
- Enunciation
- Tempo
- Organization

Materials

- Lesson 4 Concepts sheet (p. 41)
- Sets of tongue twisters for each group (pp. 42–47)

Student Objective

Students perform tongue twisters (in groups) for the class, enunciating and projecting sufficiently to be heard and understood by their peers.

Introduction

The teacher introduces the terms found on the Lesson 4 Concepts sheet.

Recognition

The teacher demonstrates these concepts by using examples and counterexamples. The students assess the teacher's performance and offer feedback.

Application

Students complete the tongue twister activity in groups.
1.   Students are divided into groups of 3–4.
2.   Each group receives a set of tongue twisters (tiered for ability).

3. Each group performs the tongue twisters for the class while applying the concepts of the lesson. The object is to say the tongue twister clearly while engaging the audience; students may use music, rhythm, movement, or any other classroom-appropriate device in their performances.

Problem Solving

Students complete individual tongue twister challenges.
1. Students write their own tongue twisters, keeping in mind any points that may have been discussed following the group challenge.
2. Students perform their individual tongue twisters for the class and receive constructive criticism, incorporating any classroom-appropriate methods and devices they like (e.g., music, rhythm).

Grade-Level Expectations

The student will:
- Read grade-appropriate material with accuracy.
- Read with appropriate silent and oral reading fluency rates, as determined by text demands and purpose.
- Read familiar texts with appropriate phrasing and expression and with attention to text features such as punctuation, italics, and dialogue.
- Demonstrate an initial understanding of the elements of literary texts by identifying literary devices as appropriate to the genre (e.g., rhyme, alliteration, simile, dialogue, imagery, simple metaphors, flashback, onomatopoeia, repetition, idioms).

Additional Notes

- Please note the following suggested timeframe for this lesson:
  o 5 min.—Gathering: 5 minutes
  o 10 min.—Introduction: 10 minutes
  o 10 min.—Preparation and rehearsal: 10 minutes
  o 20 min.—Performance: 20 minutes

- The timeframe above is for a class where students complete the group tongue twisters. If you wish, you can extend the lesson with the Problem Solving section (or have students complete this section for homework).
- Feel free to substitute your own favorite tongue twisters or to write your own (especially about topics or issues particular to your classroom). We have tiered the sets for different reading abilities: 1, 2, and 3 are for students working at grade level, 4 and 5 are for students working below grade level, and 6 is for students working above grade level. (Only one tongue twister for high-

ability students is included, but we have found that students are adequately challenged by this tongue twister.)

- You should encourage students to use expression, movement, and any other devices they can think of in their performances. Students may be reluctant at first, but they loosen up when in groups. This lesson provides you with information about which students may need some extra encouragement when it comes to performing in front of the class for the storytelling festival.

Lesson 4 Concepts

Projection

Projection is when the diaphragm is used to support the voice in order for the spoken (not yelled) word to be heard clearly by others. This is commonly taught to singers, but we rarely think about it when we speak aloud. When the speaker breathes in deeply, his or her belly should go out (instead of the shoulders going up).

Enunciation

Speaking clearly is essential to public performance. To pronounce a word distinctly, a speaker must form the consonants clearly. Pacing is important to successful enunciation. If a person is speaking too quickly, it is difficult for him or her to speak clearly.

Tone

Tone is the way somebody speaks that indicates what that person is feeling or thinking. Inflection—what a speaker emphasizes and how he or she says certain words—plays an important role in conveying tone. So does the use of descriptive words (e.g., dark, stormy, bright, sunny).

Volume

The level of sound a speaker produces is called volume. This is different from projection, which describes the mechanics of making oneself heard (through proper breathing). Volume, in terms of public speaking, refers to using a variety of vocal intensities to keep an audience's attention. An example might be a storyteller who allows his or her volume to drop during a suspenseful moment of the story, only to dramatically increase the intensity during a moment of surprise.

Tempo

The pace at which a speech or performance is delivered is called the tempo. Using the appropriate tempo allows an audience to enjoy the presentation and can be used as a cue, just like volume—during a peaceful portion of a story, the tempo may be leisurely, whereas during a more tense part, the speaker may speed up to mirror the hectic pace of events. (Alternatively, the speaker could slow down in order to be suspenseful.)

Tongue Twisters: Group #1

1.

A tree toad loved a she-toad
Who lived up in a tree.
He was a two-toed tree toad,
But a three-toed toad was she.
The two-toed tree toad tried to win
The three-toed she-toad's heart,
For the two-toed tree toad loved the ground
That the three-toed tree toad trod.
But the two-toed tree toad tried in vain.
He couldn't please her whim.
From her tree toad bower,
With her three-toed power,
The she-toad vetoed him.

2.

Whether the weather be fine, or whether the weather be not.
Whether the weather be cold, or whether the weather be hot.
We'll weather the weather, whether we like it or not.

Tongue Twisters: Group #2

1.
Mr. See owned a saw,
And Mr. Soar owned a seesaw.
Now See's saw sawed Soar's seesaw
Before Soar saw See,
Which made Soar sore.
Had Soar seen See's saw
Before See sawed Soar's seesaw,
See's saw would not have sawed
Soar's seesaw.
So See's saw sawed Soar's seesaw.
But it was sad to see Soar so sore
Just because See's saw sawed
Soar's seesaw!

2.
When a doctor doctors a doctor,
Does the doctor doing the doctoring doctor as the doctor
Being doctored wants to be doctored,
Or does the doctor doing the doctoring doctor as he wants to doctor?

Tongue Twisters: Group #3

1.
You've no need to light a nightlight
On a light night like tonight,
 For a nightlight's light's a slight light,
And tonight's a night that's light.
When a night's light, like tonight's light,
It is really not quite right
To light nightlights with their slight lights
On a light night like tonight.

2.
Say this sharply, say this sweetly,
Say this shortly, say this softly.
Say this sixteen times in succession.

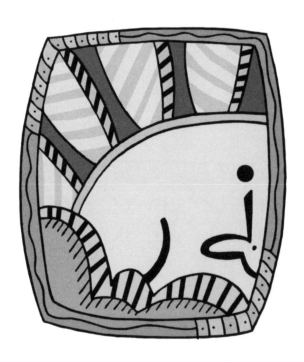

Tongue Twisters: Group #4

1.
I thought a thought.
But the thought I thought wasn't the thought I thought I thought.
If the thought I thought I thought had been the thought I thought, I wouldn't have thought so much.

2.
Can you imagine an imaginary menagerie manager
Imagining managing an imaginary menagerie?

Tongue Twisters: Group #5

1.

Bitty Batter bought some butter,
"But," said she, "This butter's bitter.
If I put it in my batter,
It will make my batter bitter."
So she bought some better butter,
And she put the better butter in the bitter batter,
And it made the bitter batter better.

2.

If a noisy noise annoys an onion, an annoying noisy noise annoys an onion more!

Tongue Twisters: Group #6

When a twister a-twisting will twist him a twist,
For the twisting of his twist, he three twines doth entwist;
But if one of the twines of the twist does untwist,
The twine that untwisteth untwisteth the twist.
Untwirling the twine that untwisteth between,
He twirls, with his twister, the two in a twine;
Then twice having twisted the twines of the twine,
He twitsteth the twist he had twined in twain.
The twain that in twining before in the twine,
As twines were entwisted he now doth untwine;
Twist the twain intertwisting a twine more between,
He, twirling his twister, makes a twist of the twine.

Lesson 5

Concepts

- Beginning, middle, and end
- Telling a story vs. acting out a story

Materials

- Storytelling cards (pp. 50–51)
- Story library of classic stories (pp. 52–73)

Student Objective

Students tell a familiar story to the class and point out the beginning, middle, and end of the story.

Introduction

The teacher discusses the differences between telling a story and acting it out. He or she should differentiate between describing the character, as one does when telling a story, and *being* a character, as one does when acting. The class can discuss how storytellers and performers use similar strategies in different ways (e.g., storytellers *describe* the setting, whereas performers *react* to that setting).

Recognition

The teacher demonstrates the previously discussed differences between storytelling and acting by telling part of a story and then being the character in the story. (For example, the teacher may tell the story of Cinderella, focusing on the scene in which Cinderella is left behind as her sisters leave for the ball and ending with the arrival of her fairy godmother. After telling the story, the teacher can move through the scene again, this time speaking as Cinderella, modifying posture, gestures, and emotion throughout the scene and becoming the character.) Students identify and discuss the differences between the told version and the acted version.

Application

Students work in groups to retell familiar stories.

1. Students work in small groups of 3–5. (These groups can be determined by the teacher or chosen by the students.)
2. Each group chooses a card with a familiar story on it. Groups may reference these stories as needed if the teacher decides to make the stories available.
3. Groups are given 5–10 minutes to discuss the elements of the story and decide how they will tell the story. (They are not reinventing the story, but rather deciding how to tell the story—without acting it out.)
4. Stories are told, and the class offers constructive criticism.

Problem Solving

Students apply the concepts of constructive criticism.

1. Students review the constructive criticism they received within their groups.
2. Students decide how to incorporate this criticism into their original performances.
3. Students retell their stories, incorporating the constructive criticism they received and focusing on new elements (at the teacher's discretion) such as sound effects.

Grade-Level Expectations

The student will:

- Identify or describe character, setting, problem/solution, and plot, as appropriate to the text.
- Identify any significant changes in character and setting.
- Paraphrase or summarize key ideas/plot and be able to put major events in sequence as appropriate to text.
- Tell stories, give information using details, and provide a coherent conclusion.

Additional Notes

- The concept of describing the character without being the character is often very difficult for students. You may want to consider either telling a story yourself or having a storyteller visit your classroom to model this technique. Having a new face visit the classroom is engaging for students, and you can give instructions to this guest speaker/performer regarding what concepts to model during the exercise.
- In the Problem Solving section, particularly if groups do not receive very much feedback, you might make suggestions that will help students as they move into the phase of the unit in which they create and tell their own stories. We like to focus on sound effects, for example.

Storytelling Cards

The Tortoise and the Hare	*The Boy Who Cried Wolf*
The Three Little Pigs	*Goldilocks and the Three Bears*
The Three Billy Goats Gruff	*Jack and the Beanstalk*

Little Red Riding Hood

Sleeping Beauty

The Princess and the Pea

The Ugly Duckling

The Tortoise and the Hare
(Based on a tale from Aesop's Fables)

Once upon a time, in the deep and quiet forest, there lived a wise and gentle tortoise. This large tortoise moved slowly through his days, foraging for food in the cooler morning and dozing contentedly on the large warm rock by the stream in the bright sun of the afternoon. His days could not have been more delightfully peaceful, apart from one thing: the hare.

The hare was a twitchy creature, always running to and fro and talking up a storm. It should be no surprise that the hare's favorite topic was . . . himself! He was forever boasting about how fast he was and making fun of the tortoise for being such a slowpoke. One day, the gentle tortoise could not listen to this obnoxious creature for one more second.

"Now listen here, Hare, no one is invincible—even you could be beaten in a race," said the tortoise.

"Ha ha ha ha," laughed the hare. "And just who is going to beat me in a race . . . you?" The hare began to walk away, laughing, when the tortoise spoke again.

"I will accept your challenge, for I cannot tolerate your boasting for another moment."

The two creatures planned the course and arranged to meet the next day at dawn. All of the forest creatures had gathered at the starting line to watch this ill-matched pair begin their race. When the start was called, the tortoise trundled off at his usual pace down the established path. The yawning hare watched his lumbering rival waddle down the path and decided that he had plenty of time for a nap before he started to run. The hare settled down by the old oak tree and quickly fell asleep.

The tortoise kept moving, but when the hare woke an hour later and ran to the top of the first hill, the tortoise was barely halfway to the finish line. The hare decided to have some breakfast, as he knew that he could catch up to the tortoise and win the race with ease. But the combination of the food and the hot sun sent the hare back into a deep sleep, and the tortoise continued his slow progress on the course.

As the sun began to sink below the horizon, the hare woke with a start. He ran to the top of the second rise. With horror, he saw that the tortoise was only a few feet from the finish line! Off he dashed, as fast as his strong hind legs could carry him. But alas, it was to no avail, for before the hare could catch up, the tortoise had crossed the finish line, to the thunderous applause of the rest of the forest creatures. The hare crossed the finish line a moment later and collapsed into a heap before the tortoise. The tortoise looked gently at the hare and said, "Slow and steady wins the race."

Fables and Folktales © Prufrock Press Inc.

The Boy Who Cried Wolf
(Based on a tale from Aesop's Fables)

Many years ago, a tribe of people lived in the forest. Everyone in the tribe had a job to do in order for the whole group to survive. The men were the hunters, the women gathered food in the forest, and the children helped wherever they could. One of the jobs that the boys shared was to watch the band's sheep while they grazed in the meadow. They had to be very vigilant and keep an eye out for wolves that might try to attack the herd and steal a sheep. Most of the boys took this responsibility very seriously, because they understood how important the sheep were to the tribe's survival.

One boy hated the job of watching the sheep. He came to dread the days when he would have to take his turn. This boy loved to be with the people and make jokes and hear the people laugh. The idea of being alone all day long with just the sheep for company was torture for him. But he knew that he had no choice and he must take his turn with the rest. The boy vowed to find a way to bring laughter to his people even though he had to stay away all day.

As the day dawned, bringing the boy's turn to go with the sheep again, he came up with a plan. As he drove the sheep down the path and onto the meadow to forage happily for their breakfast, he watched the men go out for their hunt. The women, he knew, would be moving in the opposite direction to pick the spring berries for the day. When he was sure that everyone was spread out through the forest, he climbed to the central rock in the meadow and began to cry loudly, "Wolf! Help! Wolf!" The men came running from the north, the women hurried from the south, and even the children and elders in the village came to help the boy. When they arrived in the meadow, they found the boy laughing hysterically on the rock and pointing at all of them. "Wasn't that a wonderful joke? All of you came, but there isn't any wolf!" The boy laughed and laughed. The people sheepishly agreed that he had played a funny joke, but they did not laugh as loudly or as long as the boy. Everyone returned to their jobs, asking the boy not to disturb them again.

The boy spent the morning counting sheep and dozing in the meadow. By lunchtime, he could stand it no longer. He climbed to the rock again and cried,

"Wolf! Help! Wolf!" The men and women heard him and all came running, although this time the elders kept the children in the village. When the adults reached the meadow and found that the boy was once again playing a joke on them, they were very annoyed. The men said, "You have ruined our hunting today, and we will all go hungry tonight." And the women said, "We will have to pick the strawberries again tomorrow because of the time we have wasted coming to save you!" They all said, "Do not call us again, for we will not fall for your foolishness a third time!" All of the adults stomped back to the village.

The boy felt guilty that the tribe was upset with him. After all, he was just having a bit of fun. Didn't everyone like to laugh? What was the harm of playing a joke on people, if it was all in good fun? The boy settled down to wait out the hours until dusk, when he could return to the village with the sheep. Suddenly, he saw a few sheep on the outskirts of the herd startle and run towards him. Behind them loped a large gray wolf. The boy immediately climbed up on the rock and cried, "Wolf! Help! Wolf!" But as the wolf came closer and the sheep huddled behind the boy, he realized that no one was coming to rescue him. They all thought that he was playing his same trick again. "This time I'm not lying! There really is a wolf!" he shouted. But the boy had abused his people's trust, and they did not believe his cries until it was too late. The wolf destroyed the herd, and the boy fled.

Once you are known as a liar, there are few who will believe you—even if you are telling the truth.

The Three Little Pigs

Once upon a time, there lived at the edge of the woods a large family of pigs. One day, Mr. and Mrs. Pig sat down together and discussed the problem of space in their small home. They decided that it was time for their three oldest children to make homes of their own. They called the three pigs together and said, "Pete, Pat, and Petunia, you are our pride and joy! We have watched you grow and tried to teach you to work hard and do the right thing. It is time for you to go out into the world and make lives for yourselves." The three pigs were excited, but they were nervous about going into the woods alone. They packed their few belongings and said goodbye to their family. Mr. and Mrs. Pig gave them one last piece of advice: "Beware of the Big Bad Wolf in the woods, for he is very dangerous!" The three pigs assured their parents that they would be careful and went skipping down the trail into their new lives.

The first and oldest little pig was named Pete. He was a happy little pig who loved to play the fiddle. Pete was not especially fond of hard work. As they walked down the path, Pete spied a pile of straw. "Aha!" Pete said. "This straw is perfect for the house I am going to build!" He gathered up the straw, and quick as a wink, he threw together a house of straw. The other little pigs continued down the trail, listening to Pete's happy fiddle playing.

The second little pig was named Pat. The middle pig of the litter, Pat was not a fan of hard work, either, but he realized there was some merit in it. Pat thought Pete was being very foolish to build such a shoddy house, one made of straw. Pat spied a pile of wood further down the path and quickly claimed it for his own. The third little pig, Petunia, tried to convince him that this was little better than building a house of straw, but Pat was sure that a wooden house would be much safer than his brother's. Pat spent about a day building the wooden house and then settled in for a good nap.

Meanwhile, Petunia, the third and youngest little pig, continued down the trail. Petunia knew the value of hard work and had taken her parents' advice about the Big Bad Wolf very seriously. When she found a large pile of bricks, she decided that this was the perfect material for her house. She labored day and night for a whole week. Her siblings were very impatient with her. Pete said, "Your pounding is drowning out my fiddle playing!" Pat said, "Your pounding is disturbing my nap!" But Petunia kept at her job until she had built the strongest house she could.

No sooner had she finished her house than there came a knock on Pete's straw house door. It was the Big Bad Wolf! "Little pig, little pig, let me in!" the wolf growled.

Pete answered, "Not by the hair on my chinny chin chin!"

"Then I'll huff, and I'll puff, and I'll blow your house down!" And he huffed, and he puffed, and he blew the house down. Pete's fiddle playing was never heard again!

The Big Bad Wolf continued on to the next little pig's house. Pat heard him coming and quickly shut and locked his wooden door. "Little Pig, Little Pig, let me in."

Pat answered, "Not by the hair on my chinny chin chin!"

"Then I'll huff, and I'll puff, and I'll blow your house down!" And he huffed, and he puffed, and he huffed, and he puffed, and he blew the house down. Pat was never seen again!

The Big Bad Wolf continued on down the trail and came to the brick house of Petunia, who was safely locked inside her strong brick house. The wolf knocked on the door, yelling, "Little Pig, Little Pig, let me in."

Petunia answered, "Not by the hair on my chinny chin chin!"

"Then I'll huff, and I'll puff, and I'll blow your house down!" And he huffed, and he puffed, and he huffed, and he puffed, and he huffed, and he puffed, but he couldn't blow the house down. The wolf was furious and flew into a rage. At last, the woodsmen arrived and arrested the wolf for his evil deeds!

Goldilocks and the Three Bears

Once upon a time, there was a lovely yellow house surrounded by a white picket fence at the edge of the forest. In this house, there lived a mother and a father and their very curious little girl. This young lady had blue eyes and long, blond hair, so she was known as Goldilocks. Her parents worked hard to teach her good manners, and Goldilocks generally listened—except when her curiosity got the better of her. Sometimes her need to know something became so overwhelming that she made bad decisions and put herself in danger. This is just what happened on the day that this story takes place.

The morning began normally enough, when Goldilocks rose early and dressed herself for the day. But when she came downstairs, she discovered that her parents had not awoken yet, so there was no breakfast waiting for her. Although Goldilocks would have liked to have something to eat, she also realized that this was a perfect opportunity to go exploring on her own. This was her favorite kind of exploring to do—the kind where there was no one to tell her what she could and could not look at during her exploration. So as quickly and as quietly as she could, she lifted the latch on the front door and slipped out into the early morning at the edge of the forest.

Goldilocks walked purposefully out past the picket fence and started off down the path into the forest. The morning fog had just lifted above the trees, and the woods looked bright and shiny as the morning sun filtered through the leaves. The little girl was delighted with all of the flowers and butterflies that she saw along the path. In fact, she was so caught up in her exploration that she quite forgot that this was supposed to be a short exploration so she could be back inside the house before anyone had noticed that she was gone. Suddenly, Goldilocks came around a bend in the path and saw a delightful cottage tucked under a large oak tree.

Unbeknownst to Goldilocks, this cottage was the home of three bears. Earlier that morning, the bears had gotten up and dressed. Mama Bear had made porridge, but it had been too hot to eat. Papa Bear had decided they should take Baby Bear for a walk to the blueberry bushes while the porridge cooled. So when Goldilocks stepped up to the door and knocked, the family of bears was not at home. Now, Goldilocks knew that she should not walk into a stranger's house if nobody was at home, but it was at moments such as this that her curiosity got the better of her.

Goldilocks walked right into the bears' cottage and began to explore. In the kitchen, she found three bowls of porridge sitting on the table. Now, if you will remember, Goldilocks had not eaten breakfast before leaving her house, and she was pretty hungry by this time. She decided that whoever lived in the house certainly wouldn't mind if she helped herself. She plunked herself down in front of the largest bowl and tried a spoonful, but it was too hot! She moved to the medium-sized bowl, but it was too cold! Then Goldilocks tried the littlest bowl, which was just right, so she ate it all up.

After her breakfast, Goldilocks wandered into the living room of the cottage. There she found a large lounge chair, a medium-sized overstuffed chair, and a small rocking chair. She plopped down in the lounge chair, but it was too hard! The she tried the overstuffed chair, but it was too soft! When Goldilocks sat in the small rocking chair, it was a perfect fit, but she rocked so hard that the chair fell apart, and she fell to the floor. The girl picked herself up, dusted herself off, and decided that she would look around upstairs.

The second floor of the bears' cottage was a sleeping loft, where she found three beds: a large bed, a medium-sized bed, and a little tiny bed. Goldilocks decided that it was high time for her morning nap, so she lay down on the large bed—but it was scratchy! Then she tried the medium-sized bed, but it was too lumpy! When she lay down on the tiny bed, she felt right at home, and soon she was fast asleep.

While Goldilocks was peacefully sleeping upstairs, the family of bears returned from the blueberry bushes. Baby Bear could hardly wait to put some blueberries on his porridge. But when they sat down at the table, they gasped. Papa Bear said, "Someone has been eating my porridge!"

Mama Bear said, "Someone has been eating *my* porridge!"

Baby Bear said, "Someone has been eating *my* porridge, and ate it all up!"

Thoroughly alarmed, the bears went into the living room. Papa Bear looked at his chair and said, "Someone has been sitting in my chair!"

Mama Bear looked at her chair and said, "Someone has been sitting in *my* chair!"

Baby Bear ran to his rocking chair and wailed, "Someone has been sitting in *my* chair, and broke it all to pieces!"

Angrily, the bears marched upstairs to see if there was more damage.

Papa Bear reached his bed and said, "Someone has been sleeping in my bed!"

Mama Bear said, "Someone has been sleeping in *my* bed!"

Baby Bear said, "Someone has been sleeping in *my* bed, and there she is!"

Just at that moment, Goldilocks awoke from her nap to find three angry bears staring at her. She screamed and jumped up and ran out of the cottage. Goldilocks ran down the path and did not stop running until she was past the white picket fence and inside her own house. Her parents had been very worried about her, and she confessed the whole story. Her parents marched her back to the cottage, where she apologized and promised to fix the chair and make cookies for the bears to make amends for her rudeness. The next time that Goldilocks was tempted to give in to her overwhelming curiosity, she remembered the looks on the angry bears' faces and decided against it.

The Three Billy Goats Gruff

In a mountain valley far from here, there lived three Billy Goats, and they were all named Gruff. The Billy Goats Gruff were going to the other hillside to eat the grass so they could make themselves fat. In order to get to the other hillside, they had to cross the bridge over the stream that separated the mountains. Under the bridge lived a terrible troll.

The Billy Goats Gruff argued about who should go first. The two older Billy Goats forced the youngest to cross the dangerous bridge first so they would know if the troll was home. So the littlest Billy Goat Gruff walked down the hill to the bridge. He began to cross the bridge—"trip, trap, trip, trap, trip, trap"—when suddenly the horrible troll roared to life under the bridge, yelling, "Who's that tripping over my bridge?" With his little knees knocking in fright, the poor creature replied, "It is only I, the littlest Billy Goat. I must cross the bridge so that I can eat the grass on the other side." The troll cackled, " Now I am going to gobble you up!" But as the troll began to appear over the side of the bridge, the littlest Billy Goat cried out, "Oh, no, you don't want to eat me—I am not nearly big enough to eat. Wait for my brother. He is coming after me, and he is much bigger than I am." The troll thought about this and declared, "Very well, then, be off with you!" The littlest Billy Goat Gruff ran swiftly across the bridge to the safety of the hillside. When his bigger brothers saw him cross the bridge safely, the middle brother decided to try to cross.

The second Billy Goat Gruff scampered down the hillside and began to cross the bridge—"trip, trap, trip, trap, trip, trap." Suddenly the horrible troll roared to life under the bridge, saying, "Who's that tripping over my bridge?" With his heart in his throat, the scared goat replied, "It is only I, the second Billy Goat. I must cross the bridge so that I can eat the grass on the other side." The troll cackled, "Now I am going to gobble you up!" But as the troll began to appear over the side of the bridge, the Billy Goat cried out, "Oh, no, you don't want to eat me! I am not nearly big enough to eat. Wait for my brother. He is coming after me, and he is much bigger than I am." The troll thought about this and declared, "Very well, then, be off with you!" The middle Billy Goat Gruff ran swiftly across the bridge to join his littlest brother on the hillside.

Seeing his brothers across the valley happily eating the new grass, the oldest Billy Goat Gruff decided that he was not afraid of the terrible troll. He stomped down the hill until he came to the bridge. As he crossed the bridge—"trip, trap, trip, trap, trip, trap," the horrible troll roared to life under the bridge, saying, "Who's that tripping over my bridge?" With his equally frightening voice, the largest Billy Goat Gruff replied, "It is only I, the largest Billy Goat. I must cross the bridge so that I can eat the grass on the other side." The troll cackled, "Now I am going to gobble you up!" The Billy Goat Gruff replied, "Well, come along! I've got two spears, and I'll poke your eyeballs out at your ears; I've got two curling stones, and I'll crush you to bits, body and bones." The angry troll climbed up on the bridge to do battle with the insolent Billy Goat, but the creature's horns stabbed him and his hooves crushed him, and the largest Billy Goat Gruff threw the troll back into the water. The troll floated off down the river and was never heard from again. As for the largest Billy Goat Gruff, he joined his brothers on the green hillside, where they ate grass and grew fat for the winter.

Fables and Folktales © Prufrock Press Inc.

Jack and the Beanstalk

There once was a boy called Jack who was brave and quick witted. Sadly, Jack's father had gone on a hunting trip several years before and had disappeared. So Jack and his mother lived alone in a small cottage, and their most valuable possession was their cow, Milky White. Since Jack's father's disappearance, Jack and his mother had struggled to keep themselves fed. Slowly, they had sold off everything they could. The day came when Milky White gave them no milk, and Jack's mother said she must be sold. "Take her to market," she told Jack, "and mind you get a good price for her."

So Jack set out to market, leading Milky White by her halter. After a while, he sat down to rest by the side of the road. An old man came by and Jack told him where he was going. "Don't bother to go to the market," the old man said. "Sell your cow to me. I will pay you well. Look at these beans. They are magical beans—plant them, and overnight you will find you have the finest bean plants in the entire world. You'll be better off with these beans than with an old cow or money. Jack knew his mother would be angry but he could not resist the magic beans. He agreed to the sale. The man handed the beans to Jack and took Milky White's halter.

When Jack returned home, his mother said, "Back so soon, Jack? Did you get a good price for Milky White?" Jack told her that he had exchanged the cow for five beans, and before he could even finish his account, his mother started to shout. "You lazy, good-for-nothing boy!" she screamed. "How could you hand over our cow for old beans? What will we live on now? We shall starve to death, you stupid boy." She flung the beans through the open window and sent Jack to bed without his supper.

When Jack woke the next morning, there was a strange green light in his room. All he could see from the window was green leaves. A huge beanstalk had shot up overnight. It grew higher than he could see. Quickly, Jack got dressed and stepped out of the window right onto the beanstalk and started to climb. "The old man said the beans would grow overnight," he thought. "They must indeed be magical beans."

Higher and higher Jack climbed until at last he reached the top and found himself on a strange road. Jack followed it until he came to a great castle, where he could smell a delicious breakfast cooking. Jack was hungry. It had been a long climb, and he'd had nothing to eat since midday the day before. When he reached the door of the castle, he knocked as loudly as he could on the enormous door. He heard footsteps approaching, and then the door creaked open on its hinges. The largest woman he had ever seen, as tall as a tall tree, appeared in the doorway. She looked right and left, asking, "Well, who is it? I haven't got all day!" Jack called to her, and she looked down. "Here, boy," she called. "What are you doing? Don't you know my husband likes to eat boys for breakfast? It's lucky he hasn't come down for his breakfast yet. You must run away quickly."

"Oh, please," pleaded Jack. "I only came to ask you for a bite to eat. It smells so delicious."

Now, the giant's wife had a kind heart, so she gave Jack a bacon sandwich. He was still eating it when the ground began to shake with heavy footsteps, and a loud voice boomed, "Fee, fie, foe, fum."

"Quick, hide!" cried the giant's wife, and she pushed Jack into the oven. "After breakfast, he'll fall asleep," she whispered. "That is when you must creep away." She left the oven door open a crack so that Jack could see into the room. Again the terrible rumbling voice came: "Fee, fie, foe, fum, I smell the blood of an Englishman. Be he live or be he dead, I'll grind his bones to make my bread."

A huge giant came into the room. "Boys, boys, I smell boys," he shouted. "Wife, have I got a boy for breakfast today?"

"No, dear," she said soothingly. "You have got bacon and mushrooms. You must still be smelling the boy you ate last week." The giant sniffed the air suspiciously, but at last he sat. He wolfed down his breakfast of bacon and mushrooms, drank a great bucketful of steaming tea, and crunched up a massive slice of toast. Then he demanded that his wife bring him his golden goose. The goose was bright, like no goose Jack had ever seen before, and as Jack watched in amazement, the giant commanded the hen to lay a golden egg. And it did! Before long, the giant dropped off to sleep.

Quietly, Jack crept out of the oven. He crept over to the goose's cage and lifted the latch. After tucking the goose under his arm, Jack ran as fast as he could to the top of the beanstalk. Jack stopped to listen for sounds of the giant following him, but all he heard were snores coming from the castle. Jack tucked the frightened goose into his shirt and carefully climbed down the beanstalk. At the bottom, he found his mother, looking in amazement at the goose and the beanstalk. Jack told her of his adventures in the giant's castle, and when she examined the gold eggs the goose laid for them, she realized that he was speaking the truth.

Jack and his mother used the gold to buy food. But the day came when Jack decided to climb the beanstalk again. He was thirsty for adventure, and he was certain that there must be more treasure in the giant's castle.

It was all the same as before: the long climb, the road to the castle, the smell of breakfast, and the giant's wife. But she was not so friendly this time. "Aren't you the boy who was here before," she asked, "on the day that the goose that laid the golden eggs was stolen from under my husband's nose?"

But Jack convinced her she was wrong, and in time her heart softened again and she gave him some breakfast. Once more, as Jack was eating, the ground shuddered and the great voice boomed: "Fee, fie, foe, fum." Quickly, Jack jumped into the oven. As he entered, the giant bellowed: "Fee, fie, foe, fum, I smell the blood of an Englishman. Be he live or be he dead, I'll grind his bones to make my bread."

The giant's wife put a plate of sizzling sausages before him, telling him he must be mistaken. After breakfast, the giant commanded his wife to bring him his lady harp. She was the only thing that could comfort him over the loss of the goose. The lady harp was bright and soon filled the room with the most beautiful music Jack had ever heard. Jack had memories of this music, but he couldn't place it. Then it came to him: This lady harp had used to sing him to sleep! It must have belonged to his father.

"I must rescue the lady harp, if I can," thought Jack, and he waited until the giant fell asleep. Then he slipped out of the oven, climbed the table leg, and quickly crossed to the lady harp. She remembered him and greeted him with joy, but cautioned him about the giant. The two of them quietly climbed down to the floor, and Jack picked up the harp and ran as fast as he could to the beanstalk. Jack's mother was waiting, and when she saw the harp, she burst into tears, for she knew that her husband had disappeared after attempting to rescue the lady harp from the giant's clutches. The lady harp told them sadly that Jack's father had not survived his attempt. Hearing this, Jack's mother forbade him ever to go near the beanstalk again.

Jack and his mother now lived in great luxury. But in time, Jack's curiosity got the better of him. He decided to climb the beanstalk once more. This time he did not risk talking to the giant's wife, knowing that she would recognize him. He slipped into the kitchen when she was not looking and hid himself in the log basket. He watched the giant's wife prepare breakfast, and then he heard the giant's roar: "Fee, fie, foe, fum, I smell the blood of an Englishman. Be he live or be he dead, I'll grind his bones to make my bread."

"If it's that cheeky boy who stole your goose and

our lady harp, then I'll help you catch him," said the giant's wife. "Why don't we look in the oven? It's my guess he'll be hiding there." Jack was filled with relief that he had not chosen his old hiding place. The giant and his wife hunted high and low, but they never thought to look in the log basket. At last they gave up, and the giant sat down to breakfast.

After he had eaten, the giant carried in his bags of gold. "Counting my gold coins is the only comfort I have left," he moaned. After counting both bags, the giant pretended to fall asleep. Jack was fooled by the giant's snores and crept out of his hiding place. Jack picked up two of the bags and raced down the road towards the beanstalk. Soon he heard the giant's footsteps thundering behind him. When he reached the top of the beanstalk, Jack threw the bags and started to slither down after them.

The giant followed, and now the whole beanstalk shook and shuddered with his weight so that Jack feared for his life. At last he reached the ground, and seizing an axe, he chopped at the beanstalk with all his might. Snap!

"Look out, mother!" he called as the giant came tumbling down head first. He lay dead at their feet, the beanstalk on the ground beside him. The gold provided for Jack and his mother for many years, the lady harp brought them great joy, and the goose continued to lay golden eggs for them. They lived happily and in great comfort for a long, long time.

Little Red Riding Hood

Once upon a time, a small family lived at the edge of the woods. The family included a mother, a father, and their little girl. The father was a woodsman who worked hard in the woods all day long. The mother was a famous baker and worked hard to supply the town with her goodies. The little girl played happily in the shadow of the trees. On the other side of the woods lived the mother's mother, the little girl's grandmother. The grandmother had been a seamstress all her life and made beautiful clothes. In fact, she had made her granddaughter a bright red hooded cape, and all through the region, the little girl was known as Little Red Riding Hood.

One day, after the woodsman had left for work, the mother told Little Red Riding Hood that Grandma was not feeling well. The mother had too much work to do that day to make the journey through the woods to Grandma's house. She asked Little Red if she felt comfortable making the journey alone. Little Red was very excited, because this was the first time her mother had entrusted her to walk through the woods by herself. After packing a basket full of goodies for Grandma and putting on her red cloak, Little Red was ready. Her mother reminded her not to talk to strangers, and off went Little Red, skipping down the path into the woods.

Little Red had taken the path through the woods many times with her mother and father, so she was not worried about finding her way. She stopped to look at the beautiful flowers and to listen to the songbirds along the way. When she had gone halfway through the woods, she stopped to rest for a moment under the shade of the old oak tree that grew in the very center of the forest. As she sat and rested, she heard another creature approaching.

Unbeknownst to Little Red, she had been watched carefully as she skipped though the forest. The Big Bad Wolf was tracking the girl and was very interested in what she had in her basket. He came up the side path by the oak tree, whistling a happy tune.

"Why, it's Little Red Riding Hood," the wolf said as he neared the tree. "Those goodies in your basket smell awfully good!"

Little Red Riding Hood, remembering what her mother had told her about strangers, immediately replied, "I cannot talk to you, because I am not allowed to talk to strangers."

The wolf laughed his best carefree laugh and said, "Oh, don't be silly. I am not a stranger—why, I have known your parents for years! I remember the day you were born."

"Well in that case," said Little Red Riding Hood, "I suppose I could share a biscuit with you, but I mustn't give you any more than one. These are for my grandmother, who lives on the other side of the woods." The wolf gobbled down his biscuit, thanked Little Red, and told her to be careful as she finished her journey.

"There are many creatures in the woods who would love to gobble you up, just as I gobbled up your mother's biscuits!" Little Red was uncomfortable around the wolf and happily left him to complete her walk to her grandmother's house.

As soon as she was out of sight, the wolf set off through the woods and took a shortcut to the old woman's cottage. Wasting no time, he walked right in and shut Grandma up in the closet. The wolf quickly put on one of Grandma's nightgowns and a sleeping bonnet and got into her bed. He was just pulling the covers up to his large nose when he heard Little Red come into the house. Little Red called out, "Hello, Grandma, I have brought you some goodies from my mother's kitchen. May I come in?"

The wolf pitched his voice as high as he could and replied, "Why of course, my dear." Little Red came into the bedroom and approached the bed.

She looked down and said, "Why Grandma, what big eyes you have."

The wolf replied, "The better to see you with, my dear."

"Why, Grandma," said Little Red, "what big ears you have."

"The better to hear you with, my dear," said the wolf.

With a growing sense of alarm, Little Red said, "Why Grandma, what big teeth you have."

The wolf yelled, "The better to eat you with, my dear!" And he leapt from the bed and chased Little Red around the house, fully intending to gobble her up. Little Red's screams reached the ears of her father, who was working nearby. He came running just in time to save Little Red and chase the wolf off into the woods. The father and daughter quickly freed Grandma from the closet. The woodsman was relieved that both Grandma and Little Red were all right. Grandma was furious with the wolf for stealing her favorite nightgown—and Little Red promised never to talk to strangers again!

Sleeping Beauty

A long, long time ago, there were a king and queen who longed to have child. But the years went by, and they never had one. One day the queen was bathing in the river, and a frog crept from the water up onto the land, and he said to her, "Your wish shall be fulfilled, for before a year has gone by, you shall have a daughter."

What the frog had said came true, and the queen had a little girl who was so wonderful that the king wanted to show her off to everyone in the land, so he ordered a great feast. He invited not only his kin, friends, and acquaintances, but also the wise women, in order that they might be kind and well disposed toward the child. There were 13 wise women in his kingdom, but the king invited only 12 of the women. The final wise woman was the nastiest person he had ever met, and he did not want her to be anywhere near his perfect daughter.

The stupendous feast was held, and when it came to an end, the wise women bestowed their magic gifts upon the baby—one gave virtue, another beauty, a third riches, and so on, so that the child was blessed with every gift that anybody could ever wish for. Each of the wise women tried to outdo the one who came before her, giving the finest and most cherished gift possible.

When 11 of the wise women had given their gifts, the uninvited wise woman burst into the great hall. She was furious that she had not been invited, and she was bound for vengeance. She looked wildly around the great hall, her face and voice filled with rage, and she cried, "When she is 18, the princess shall prick herself with a spindle, and she shall fall down dead." And then, without saying another word, she turned around and left the room.

The guests and the royal family were all shocked, but the last wise woman, whose good wish remained unspoken, came forward. Finally she spoke, saying, "A powerful curse has been lain on the princess, one that I cannot fully undo—but it shall not be death that strikes the princess once the spindle pierces her skin, but a deep sleep of 100 years. And when this comes to pass, her entire household will sleep alongside her, so that her family and friends will not be forced to live without her light."

The king, in an effort to keep his dear child from the foretold misfortune, gave orders that every spindle in the entire kingdom should be burnt. Meanwhile, the gifts of the wise women blossomed in the princess, who was so smart, so kind, and so fair that all who knew her could not help but love her.

On the day the princess turned 18, the king and queen were busy making plans to celebrate her birthday. They did not notice when the maiden wandered off to explore the palace on her own. The princess looked curiously into all sorts of places—looked into unused rooms and bedchambers and closets—and at last came to an old tower. She climbed up the narrow, winding staircase, and she reached a little door. A rusty key stood ready in the lock, and when she turned it, the door sprang open. There, in the center of the little room, sat an old woman with a spindle, busily spinning her flax.

"Good day," said the king's daughter. "May I ask what you are doing?"

"I am spinning," said the old woman, nodding her head.

"What sort of contraption is that, rattling round so merrily?" asked the girl, who of course had never seen a spindle. She moved towards it, wanting to try it for herself. But no sooner had she touched the spindle than the magic decree was fulfilled. The princess felt the needle prick her skin, and in an instant, she fell upon the bed and drifted into a deep, immovable sleep. This blackest sleep extended over all of the palace, so that the king and queen fell down together into slumber on the stone floor of the great hall, and the whole of the court lay down beside them. The horses went to sleep in the stable, the dogs lay motionless in the yard, the pigeons were still in their coops, the flies were frozen to the windowpanes, and even the fire that had been roaring in the hearth stopped, its flames caught in their leaping. The wind fell silent, and the leaves would not so much as tremble on their branches.

Around the silent castle there began to grow a hedge of thorns. Every year the hedge crept higher, and at last the thorny stalks grew up over the walls and laced together so that the castle was enshrouded, utterly hidden from view.

But people throughout the land whispered the story of Briar Rose, the perfect princess sleeping in the center of the thorn-covered castle. From time to time, kings' sons came and tried to hack through the thorny fence. But they found it impossible, for the thorns held fast, like hands grasped determinedly together—and those youths who tried too long became trapped in the thorns, never to be seen again.

After many, many years, a king's son came again to that country, and this prince heard an old man talking about the thorn hedge, and about the wonderful princess, Briar Rose, who slept within the castle buried beneath the treacherous thorns, and about her family and servants who slumbered all around her. The old man told the prince that many kings' sons had already come and tried to fight through the thorny hedge, and had died pitiable deaths.

But this youth declared, "I am not afraid. I will go and see this Briar Rose." The old man, try as he might, could not dissuade the enthusiastic prince.

When the king's son approached the castle, there were no thorns in sight, but rather a wall of beautiful, fragrant flowers, which parted as if to allow him in and closed gently behind him as he passed. It was the hundredth anniversary of the princess having pricked her finger, and the time had come for her and her household to be released from their prison of dreaming. In the castle yard, the prince saw the horses and the spotted hounds lying asleep, and he saw the pigeons curled under their wings in the coops. When he entered the house, the flies were yet frozen to the windows. The prince gazed in wonder at this strange enchantment, but he kept going.

He went on farther, and in the great hall, he saw the whole of the court lying asleep, with the king and queen stretched out on the floor beside their thrones. He walked on and on, exploring the same rooms that Briar Rose had explored on her fateful birthday, until he found her. There she lay, looking peaceful and wonderful, and the prince knew at once that he loved her. He bent down and kissed her, and at that moment she woke up.

When the prince and princess went down together to the great hall, they found the king and queen and courtesans—all of them still quite groggy. The horses in the courtyard stood up and shook out their manes, the hounds jumped up and wagged their tails, the flames leapt to life in the fireplace, the flies went off in search of unguarded food, and the leaves on the trees shook slightly in the light wind.

The prince and Briar Rose were married, and for the rest of their days they made each other very happy and ruled fairly and kindly over the land.

The Princess and the Pea
(From Hans Christian Andersen)

Once upon a time, there was a prince who wanted to find a princess, but he was determined that she should be a *real* princess. So he traveled all around the world to find one, but he was never satisfied. There were many princesses, but the prince could never be completely sure that they were real princesses who deserved his love. There was always something about them that was not quite right. He became very discouraged, thinking that he would never find what he was looking for. His mother, the queen, tried to cheer him up, saying that she would try to help him find a bride.

One evening there was a terrible storm. Lightning flashed in the castle's windows, and thunder made its stone walls vibrate. The rain poured down, flooding the moat. During a lull in the roaring thunder, a loud knock sounded on the door. A bedraggled woman was let in. She looked a fright, with stringy hair and rain-soaked clothing. Water ran from her shoes and dripped from her hands. She told the queen, who came to inquire after her, that she was a princess.

"Well, we shall soon find out what you are," thought the old queen. But she said nothing, went into the bedroom, removed all of the bedding, and laid a pea on the bottom of the bed. Then she took 20 mattresses and laid them on top of one another, with the pea on the very bottom, and then put 20 featherbeds of eiderdown on top of the mattresses.

This was where the strange woman was allowed to sleep for the night. She thought it very strange to have to sleep on top of so many mattresses and featherbeds, but she was much too polite to say anything, so she climbed a ladder and got into bed and went to sleep.

In the morning, the queen asked how the woman had slept.

"Oh," said the woman. "I don't mean anything against your kind hospitality, but I slept horribly!" she said. "I hardly closed my eyes all night. There was something disrupting my sleep. It was something hard, and my back aches today!"

The queen knew all too well that this woman must be a true princess, for only a princess would make such a great big fuss about a little old pea. So she introduced the princess to her son and told him that this, at last, was a true princess. The prince was delighted, and he wed the princess soon thereafter. They got along perfectly, and the queen was satisfied that she had made her son happy. The pea, incidentally, was put into the royal art gallery, where it can still be seen—unless somebody has taken it.

The Ugly Duckling
(From Hans Christian Andersen)

Once upon a time, down on an old farm, there lived a duck family. Mother Duck had been sitting on a clutch of new eggs. One nice morning, the eggs hatched, and out popped six chirpy ducklings. But one egg, which was bigger than the rest, didn't hatch. Mother Duck couldn't recall laying that seventh egg. How had it gotten there? Tock! Tock! The little prisoner was pecking on the inside of his shell, impatient to escape.

"Did I count the eggs wrong?" Mother Duck wondered. But before she could worry about it for too long, the last egg finally hatched. A strange-looking duckling emerged, one with gray feathers that should have been yellow. It moved differently than its brothers and sisters, and it had a gangly neck. The duckling gazed up at its worried mother.

Though she tried to keep herself from thinking such thoughts, she couldn't help but wonder about the duckling. "I can't understand how this ugly duckling can be one of mine!" she said to herself, shaking her head as she looked at her lastborn duckling.

This gray duckling ate far more than his siblings, and he outgrew them, becoming very large. As the days went by, the poor ugly duckling became more and more unhappy. His siblings didn't want to play with him because he was so clumsy, and all of the farmyard folks simply laughed at him. He felt sad and lonely, although Mother Duck did her best to console him.

"Poor ugly duckling!" she would say to herself. "Why must he be so different from the others?" And the ugly duckling felt worse than ever. He secretly wept at night. He felt as though nobody wanted him.

"Nobody loves me, and they all tease me! Why am I different from my brothers and sisters?" he sobbed quietly.

The day came when the ugly duckling could not bear it anymore and felt he must take action. One morning, when the sun was just beginning to rise, he ran away from the farmyard. He stopped at a pond and began to question all of the other birds.

"Do you know of any other ducklings with gray feathers like mine?" Everybody he asked shook their heads in scorn.

"We don't know anyone as ugly as you," they said meanly.

The ugly duckling did not lose heart, however, and he kept on making inquiries. He went to another pond, where a pair of large geese gave him the same answer as the other birds had. Even worse, they warned him to leave at once. "Don't stay here! It's dangerous. There are men with guns around here!" The duckling began to feel sorry that he had ever left the farmyard.

Then one day, the ugly duckling's travels took him near an old countrywoman's cottage. Thinking that he was a stray goose, she caught him. "I'll put this in a hutch. I hope it's a female and lays plenty of eggs!" said the old woman, whose eyesight was poor. But the ugly duckling laid not a single egg, of course, and the hen kept frightening him.

"Just wait!" said the hen. "If you don't lay any eggs, the old woman will wring your neck and pop you into the pot!"

And the cat chipped in, "Hee! Hee! I hope the woman cooks you so that I can gnaw at your bones!"

The poor ugly duckling was so scared that he lost his appetite, although the old woman kept stuffing him with food and grumbling, "If you won't lay eggs, then at least hurry up and get plump so that I can eat you!"

"Oh, dear me!" moaned the now-terrified duckling. "I'll die of fright first! And I'll die knowing that nobody ever loved me!"

But one night, finding the hutch door ajar, the ugly duckling escaped. Once again he was all by himself. He ran as far away as he could, and at dawn, he found himself in a thick bed of reeds. "If nobody wants me, I suppose I'll hide here forever," he thought. There was plenty of food, and the duckling began to feel a little happier, despite being terribly lonely. One day at sunrise, he saw a flock of beautiful birds moving across the sky. They were white, with long, slender necks, yellow beaks, and large wings, and they were migrating south.

"If only I could look like one of those birds, even if only for a day!" said the ugly duckling admiringly. Winter came, and the water in the reed bed froze. The poor duckling tried to seek food in the snow, but he had no luck, and eventually he wore himself out completely. He dropped exhausted to the ground, where a farmer found him and put him in his big jacket pocket, saying, "I'll take him home to my children. They'll look after him. Poor thing, he's frozen!" At the farmer's house, the farmer's children showered the ugly duckling with kindly care and fawned over him. The children had saved the duckling from the bitterly cold winter.

By the time spring had come, the ugly duckling had grown so large that the farmer decided to set him free next to the pond, where the farmer thought there would be plenty of food for him to eat.

When the ugly duckling walked up to the pond, he was taken aback upon seeing his own reflection. "Goodness," he thought to himself. "How I've changed! I hardly recognize myself."

Just at that moment, the ugly duckling heard a faint noise in the distance. It grew stronger, the sound of many beating wings, and the ugly duckling was pleased to see a flock of the same beautiful birds he'd once seen passing overhead. To his delight, the birds began to land on the pond to drink. When the birds came near enough for the ugly duckling to see them up close, he was shocked to see that they looked just like him.

"Ah," one of the beautiful birds said. "A fellow swan!"

"A what?" the ugly duckling asked, very confused.

"Why, a swan, of course," said the beautiful bird. "That's what you are. A swan—although perhaps a rather silly one! Are you alone? Where have you been hiding, and how did you survive the terrible winter?"

"It's a long story," replied the beautiful young swan, still astounded.

The other swans were glad to add another member to their numbers. Now, the beautiful young swan swam and flew majestically with his fellow swans. One day, he heard a child on the riverbank exclaim, "Look at that young swan! Look how lovely he is." And the young swan knew that it was true.

Lesson 6

Concepts

- Moral of a story
- Symbolism

Materials

- Fables and Folktales Final Project sheet (p. 77)
- Lesson 6 Concepts sheet (p. 78)
- Character sheets (pp. 79–80)
- Plot sheet (p. 81)
- Planning sheets (pp. 82–84)

Student Objective

Students are provided with complete information about the authentic performance assessment project by reading over and discussing the materials listed above.

Introduction

The teacher and students read aloud the prompt for the authentic performance assessment (the final project), reviewing the terms on the Lesson 6 Concepts sheet.

Recognition

The class reflects upon and discusses the following questions:

- How old will you be in 2060? What kind of wisdom do you think you will have by then?
- What are the rules in your life that are important to you? How does this relate to morals and messages?
- What is symbolism? What are universal themes?

Application

Distribute the Character sheet, the Plot sheet, and the Planning sheets and review the content.

1. Stress that students must complete the Planning sheets and have them approved by the designated date.
2. Answer any questions and address any concerns that students may have.

Problem Solving

Students begin planning for the authentic performance project.

1. Students should begin completing their Planning sheets.
2. At the teacher's discretion, students have the option of working with a partner. (If this option is chosen, then students must approach the teacher and persuade him or her that the partnership would result in an improved final project for both parties.)

Grade-Level Expectations

The student will:

- Read grade-appropriate material with accuracy.
- Read with appropriate silent and oral fluency rates.
- Identify the meaning of unfamiliar vocabulary by using strategies to unlock meaning.
- Show breadth of vocabulary knowledge, demonstrating understanding of word meanings and relationships by selecting appropriate words or explaining the use of words in context, including content-specific vocabulary, words with multiple meanings, and precise vocabulary.

Additional Notes

- Keep the following skills in mind as you observe your students at work. You might discuss specific concepts and issues with them as you see how they are progressing in their planning:
  - o creating a story with a message/purpose;
  - o sequencing a story in a way that is easy for listeners to follow;
  - o using symbolism in storytelling effectively;
  - o using colorful nouns, verbs, adjectives, and adverbs appropriately;
  - o varying the tone and volume of their voices to add drama to their storytelling; and
  - o completing the project on time.

  Make it clear that participation is mandatory. Throughout the unit, there have been opportunities for students to perform and present in front of the class, the hope being that by this point, they are comfortable. If you have a student with extreme circumstances, of course, you can make whatever adaptations are most helpful. We had a student with emotional issues that prevented him from being able to present, so we allowed him to create a movie that he brought in.

- It is preferable for students to tell their stories from memory. However, teacher discretion can be used when it comes to those students you think may need the crutch of note cards. Warn students who are allowed to use note cards that this could cause them to have less eye contact and focus, potentially making their presentations less engaging.

- Time management may be the biggest challenge of all for some of your students. It is important that students work on their stories in class. Remind them that they will have a limited amount of time during which to work on this project, so they will need to use their time wisely. Review the due dates and check point dates for the project with the class.

- You should think carefully about whether or not you will allow students to work with partners for the authentic performance project. The pros of allowing partner projects include that students sometimes brainstorm better with others and have more confidence in mutual decisions, they have somebody with whom to share the work load, and they have additional performance options—for instance, one person could narrate the story while the other provided background, miming, and sound effects. The cons of allowing partners include that the partners could distract each other, they could distribute or complete work unevenly, and an absence on the part of one partner could negatively affect the other partner's progress. It is up to you whether to allow students to choose their own partners, obtain teacher approval, and so forth.

Fables and Folktales Final Project

A good storyteller grabs the imagination of his or her audience and holds listeners captive with his or her tale. You have learned about fables and different types of folktales—trickster tales, how and why stories, and so on. Now it is time to weave your own magic.

Here is the situation: The year is 2060. You have lived a long life and have learned much along the way. A teacher at a local middle school has invited you to participate in the annual storytelling festival hosted by the school. You must create your own fable or folktale to share with the students.

In the process of developing your story, you will need to ask yourself a number of questions, including the following:

- What type of story do I want to tell?
- What message/moral/explanation/advice do I want my story to give to listeners?
- How will I use symbolism to connect my story to universal themes that transcend time and/or place?
- Do I want to modernize or revise an old story, or create a brand-new one?
- Who will my characters be, and what will they be like?
- What will my story be about?
- How will my story unfold? What will happen first? What will happen after that?
- What storytelling techniques will I use to share my story with others?

As you decide how to answer these questions, record your ideas on the Planning sheet provided. Once you have completed this form, have the teacher look over and initial it to confirm that you are ready to put the pieces together into a well-crafted story.

As you develop the story itself, think about how you can make the words that you use, the details that you include, and the expressiveness of your voice make the tale you tell more interesting and exciting.

The storytelling festival is scheduled to take place on _____.
Come prepared—your work will be evaluated using a rubric that you will go over in class.

This prompt was developed by Drs. Moon, Callahan, Brighton, and Tomlinson under the auspices of the National Research Center. All permissions secured.

Lesson 6 Concepts

Vocabulary

Moral/Message: This is the lesson the story teaches—for example, Goldilocks learned to listen to her parents and not go into strangers' houses uninvited.

Symbolism: Symbolism involves using items or characters in your story to represent larger ideas, concepts, and lessons. For instance, wolves often represent evil, such as in *Little Red Riding Hood*.

Universal Theme: This refers to a message or component of the story that is understood by everybody—it is not an inside joke or a cultural reference, which only certain people in certain places (or in certain time periods) would understand. Examples of universal themes include the love of a parent for a child, the horrors of war, and so on.

Things to Keep in Mind

You will need to practice time management. For the final project, you will have a limited amount of time to work, so you need to use your time wisely. Review the due dates and check point dates with the teacher, and keep them in mind.

You may decide to work with a partner. The pros of working with a partner on your project include that partners sometimes brainstorm better together and are more confident in their decisions, they have somebody with whom to share the work load, and they have additional performance options—for instance, one person could narrate the story while the other provided background, miming, and sound effects.

The cons of working with partners include that the partners could distract each other, they could distribute or complete work unevenly, and if one person were absent, it could negatively affect the other person's progress.

Name:_____ Date:_____

Character

Character's Name:_____

1. What does this character **think**?

   _____

   _____

   _____

2. What does this character **do**?

   _____

   _____

   _____

3. What does this character **say**?

   _____

   _____

   _____

4. What does this character **feel**?

_____

_____

_____

5. Where does this character **go**?

_____

_____

_____

6. What is this character's **goal**?

_____

_____

_____

Fables and Folktales © Prufrock Press Inc.

Name:_____ Date: _____

Plot

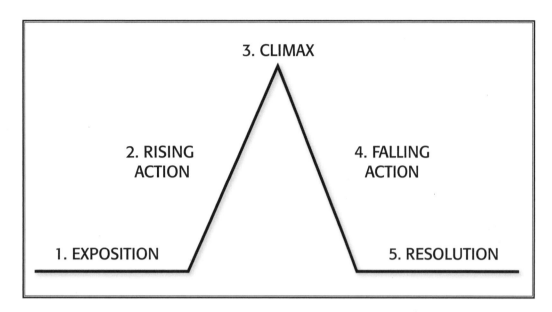

3. CLIMAX

2. RISING ACTION

4. FALLING ACTION

1. EXPOSITION

5. RESOLUTION

FILL IN YOUR PLOT OUTLINE.

1. _____

_____

2. _____

_____

3. _____

_____

4. _____

_____

5. _____

_____

Name:_____ Date: _____

Planning

Type of Story

Part 1 (check all that apply)

- ❑ Fable
- ❑ Trickster tale
- ❑ How and why story
- ❑ Fairytale
- ❑ Other (specify)

Part 2 (check one)

- ❑ Modernization or revision of old story
- ❑ Brand-new story

Main point, message, or theme:

_____

_____

_____

_____

Characters:

Name	Physical Description	Personality and Characteristics

Plot summary: (Briefly, what will your story be about?)

_____

_____

_____

_____

Sequence of events: (Step-by-step, what will happen in your story?)

1. _____

   _____

   _____

2. _____

   _____

   _____

3. _____

   _____

   _____

4. _____

   _____

   _____

5. _____

   _____

   _____

Fables and Folktales © Prufrock Press Inc.

Permission is granted to photocopy or reproduce this page for single classroom use only.

83

6. _____

_____

_____

Planning sheets completed on: _____

Teacher's signature:_____

Fables and Folktales © Prufrock Press Inc.

Lesson 7

Concepts
- Time management and meeting deadlines
- The importance of purpose, sequencing, symbolism, word usage, and expression

Materials
- Student portfolios
- Rubric sheets (p. 87)
- Story prompt cards (printed and laminated; pp. 88–92)

Student Objective
Students continue and complete their planning for the authentic performance project, keeping in mind the criteria listed on the rubric.

Introduction
The teacher reviews and discusses the provided scoring rubric with students.

Recognition
Students give examples of a successful story (crafted by a wondrous wordsmith) and compare it to examples of a less successful story (crafted by a tale teller in training).

Application
Students work and receive assistance as necessary.
1. Students continue to plan their stories alone or with a partner.

2. The teacher circulates and meets with individuals or pairs of students, using the story prompt cards as a resource for students who are having difficulty at different points of the process.

Problem Solving

Students demonstrate an understanding of the scoring rubric.

1. Students write their own rubric using the six areas of focus: purpose, sequencing, symbolism, word usage, expressiveness, and timeliness.
2. Students ask questions and discuss examples while crafting their rubrics if they experience confusion.

Grade-Level Expectations

The student will:

- Identify or describe character, setting, problem/solution, and plot, as appropriate to the text, and identify any significant changes in character and setting.
- Paraphrase or summarize key ideas/plot points, with major events sequenced, as appropriate to the text.
- Tell stories, give information using details, and provide a coherent conclusion.

Additional Notes

- It is important to clearly explain both the task (the authentic performance project) and the scoring rubric to students. As each component of the rubric is explained, solicit and/or provide illustrations of quality performance, drawing examples from the stories students have read or listened to in class.
- The Problem Solving section, wherein students create their own rubrics, is provided as an option for higher ability students.
- The story prompt cards are very effective in reenergizing and redirecting students when they get stuck. They also send a message of resourcefulness, letting students know that when they are confused, it is within their power to use the resources available to them and to continue working.
- As you move around the room, you will notice which students are on track and which are falling behind and may need more careful monitoring. Students who seem confused occasionally are actually simply less inclined to perform in front of the class and are procrastinating; you can work with these students to discuss how they might present their stories in a way that is not intimidating.

Rubric

		Wondrous Wordsmith (3 Points)	Skillful Storyteller (2 points)	Tale Teller in Training (1 point)
PURPOSE	Score: ___	The story you tell clearly and powerfully leads your listener to understand and appreciate the main idea/message.	The listener is able to understand the purpose of your story.	The main point of your story is unclear. The listener is left unsure of the message you are trying to get across.
SEQUENCING	Score: ___	You effortlessly lead your listener along your story's path—from the introduction of the characters to the final resolution of conflict.	There are minor inconsistencies or gaps in the sequencing of your story. Still, listeners are able to understand and follow the basic series of events.	The listener is unable to follow your story. The sequence of events that you use is illogical or overly complicated.
SYMBOLISM	Score: ___	Characters and events in your story are clearly symbolic of people and happenings across time and/or place.	You use symbolism to represent people or happenings, but the symbolism does not easily transfer or connect to other times and/or places.	There is little or no symbolism apparent in your story, or the symbolism does not transfer to other times and/or places.
WORD USAGE	Score: ___	You use vivid and powerful nouns, verbs, adjectives, and adverbs when telling your story. The listener can visualize in detail what happens.	You use nouns, verbs, adjectives, and adverbs appropriately to express your ideas. The listener is able to picture events or people in your story.	You do not make appropriate use of nouns, verbs, adjectives, and adverbs. The listener is unable to visualize people or events in your story.
EXPRESSIVENESS	Score: ___	Your story comes to life as you speak clearly and vary the tone and volume of your voice to match what is happening in your story.	Your voice is clear as you tell your story, but you do not vary your tone of voice and/or volume in a way that captivates and holds the listener's attention.	It is difficult to hear or understand you as you tell the story. You do not vary your volume or tone of voice.
TIMELINESS	Score: ___	You are well prepared and present your story at the festival as scheduled.	You are not prepared to present your story at the scheduled time, but you present it within 1–2 days.	You are not prepared to present your story at the scheduled time or within 2 days of the festival, or you do not tell a story.

This rubric was developed by Drs. Moon, Callahan, Brighton, and Tomlinson under the auspices of the National Research Center. All permissions secured.

TYPE OF STORY

Does your story have
a main character who
likes to trick others?

Does the character trick
others to get his or her way?

Does the character
lose in the end?

Then your story is a
TRICKSTER TALE.

TYPE OF STORY

Is your story about a natural
feature or occurrence,
such as hurricanes,
mountains, or the sun?

Does your story tell
why or how this natural
thing occurred or came
into the world?

Is your story made up,
rather than scientific?

Then your story is a
HOW AND WHY STORY.

TYPE OF STORY

Are the characters in your
story going to be animals?

Will you provide the
audience with a message
or moral at the end?

Is the plot simple?

Then your story is a FABLE.

TYPE OF STORY

Is your plot complicated?

Do any of your characters
use magic in the story?

Does your story use
magic or enchantment
to solve the problem?

Then your story is
a FAIRYTALE.

THEME

Where do you want to be
when you're 18 years old?

What do you need to
do to get there?

What inspires you?

THEME

What is the one thing you
would never do to a friend?

What would you tell
somebody who was new
to your neighborhood?

How do you tell who
your real friends are?

THEME

How do you solve most
problems (or important
problems) in your life?

What is the most
important thing a person
should do every day?

If you could give somebody
a piece of advice to improve
daily life, what would it be?

THEME

What is the most important
thing your parent or
guardian has taught you?

What is the most
important rule in your
house/classroom?

What does your coach
tell you at practice?

CHARACTER

How old is your character?

What color hair does
your character have?

Is your character tall?

CHARACTER

Is your character based
on somebody you know?

Draw a picture of
your character and
describe him or her.

Make a list of adjectives to
describe your character.

CHARACTER

Is your character an
animal? What kind? Why?

What color fur (or if not
fur, scales, skin, and so on)
does your character have?

How does your character
move? Does it crawl,
walk, fly, or swim?

CHARACTER

Is your character brave?

Does your character
always know what he
or she is doing?

Is your character foolish?

SETTING

Close your eyes and imagine the place where the story occurs.

Does your story take place inside or outside?

Is there more than one setting or place in your story?

SETTING

If your story takes place inside, how big is the space?

Is this a specific kind of indoor place (such as a home, a school, or a store)?

What type of furniture is there in this space?

SETTING

If your story takes place outside, is it hot or cold in this place?

It this place in the country or in the city?

What does it sound like in this place?

SETTING

Draw a picture of the place where your story happens.

Describe your picture using as many vivid adjectives as you can.

What is the mood of this place?

PLOT

Is the problem in your story caused by the place (e.g., a haunted house, a volcano)?

Is the problem caused by one character?

Does the problem affect everyone in the story?

PLOT

Is the problem something to be overcome or a problem that needs to be solved?

Is it a problem that happens to everyone? Is it a once-in-a-lifetime kind of issue?

Has this problem ever happened to you?

PLOT

How do the characters find out about the problem?

Do they see the problem as intimidating, or as a challenge?

Do they panic or remain calm?

PLOT

Does your story have a hero who solves the problem alone?

Is the solution a group effort?

How does the solution teach the moral of the story?

Fables and Folktales © Prufrock Press Inc.

Lesson 8

Concepts
- Storytelling techniques
- Differences between storytelling and acting

Materials
- Sample story with storytelling techniques (pp. 95–96)
- Story library (pp. 52–73)

Student Objective

Students understand, experience, and utilize storytelling techniques.

Introduction

The teacher uses the sample story and cues to demonstrate the techniques of repeating a word or refrain, stressing certain words, changing volume, using sound effects, modifying facial expressions, and making deliberate eye contact.

Recognition

After hearing the sample story, students are asked to identify some of the techniques, explain how they were used, and discuss how the story would have been different without those techniques, as well as how the story would have been different had it been acted out instead of told.

Application

Students work in pairs to practice the lesson's concepts.
1. Each pair chooses one of the familiar narratives provided in the story library.
2. After reading through their chosen narratives, students choose 2–3 techniques to use with the story.

3.   After writing cues for themselves into the stories, they practice telling the story to their partners.

Problem Solving

Students take their own stories (for the storytelling festival) and insert or highlight where they can use some of the techniques that have been demonstrated and practiced.

Grade-Level Expectations

The student will:
- Demonstrate an initial understanding of the elements of literary texts by identifying or describing character(s), setting, problem/solution, and plot, as appropriate to the text, and by identifying any significant changes in character and setting over time.
- Analyze and interpret elements of literary texts, citing evidence where appropriate, by describing characters' traits, motivations, and interactions and citing thoughts, words, and actions that reveal characters' traits, motivations, and changes over time.
- Demonstrate an initial understanding of elements of literary texts by identifying the characteristics of a variety of types/genres of literary texts (e.g., poetry, plays, fairytales, fantasy, fables, realistic fiction, folktales, historical fiction, mysteries, science fiction, myths, legends).
- Analyze and interpret elements of literary texts, citing evidence where appropriate, by making inferences about cause/effect, external conflicts (e.g., person versus person, person versus nature/society/fate), and the relationships among elements within text (e.g., how the historical era influences the characters' actions or thinking).

Additional Notes

- There is a subtle but important difference between acting out a story and telling a story. We have found that this is often the hardest concept for students to grasp in this unit. Modeling the storytelling techniques is essential for students to do in order to understand that they need to employ facial expressions, sound effects, and other methods in order to portray characters without actually *becoming* those characters.
- Remember that these stories are just for practice—there is no need for students to memorize them or for their performances to be perfect. The object is to encourage the students to experiment with the techniques. The ultimate goal is for students to become comfortable using these techniques and for them to consider how they might use these same techniques when telling their stories.

Sample Story: The Three Billy Goats Gruff

In a mountain valley far from here, there lived three Billy Goats, and they were all named Gruff (GRRUUFF). The Billy Goats Gruff (GRRUUFF) were going to the other hillside to eat the grass so they could make themselves fat. In order to get to the other hillside, they had to cross the bridge over the stream that separated the mountains. Under the bridge lived a terrible troll (SCARY FACE).

The Billy Goats Gruff (GRRUUFF) argued about who should go first. The two older Billy Goats forced the youngest to cross the dangerous bridge first so they would know if the troll was home. So the littlest Billy Goat Gruff (GRRUUFF) walked down the hill to the bridge. He began to cross the bridge—"trip, trap, trip, trap, trip, trap" (DRUM BEATS)—when suddenly the horrible troll (SCARY FACE) roared to life under the bridge, yelling (LOUD VOICE), "Who's that tripping over my bridge?" With his little knees knocking in fright, the poor creature replied (HIGH VOICE), "It is only I, the littlest Billy Goat. I must cross the bridge so that I can eat the grass on the other side." The troll (SCARY FACE) cackled (LOUD VOICE), " Now I am going to gobble you up!" But as the troll (SCARY FACE) began to appear over the side of the bridge, the littlest Billy Goat cried out (HIGH VOICE), "Oh, no, you don't want to eat me—I am not nearly big enough to eat. Wait for my brother. He is coming after me, and he is much bigger than I am." The troll (SCARY FACE) thought about this and declared (LOUD VOICE), "Very well, then, be off with you!" The littlest Billy Goat Gruff (GRRUUFF) ran swiftly across the bridge to the safety of the hillside. When his bigger brothers saw him cross the bridge safely, the middle brother decided to try to cross.

The second Billy Goat Gruff (GRRUUFF) scampered down the hillside and began to cross the bridge—"trip, trap, trip, trap, trip, trap" (DRUM BEATS). Suddenly the horrible troll (SCARY FACE) roared to life under the bridge, saying (LOUD VOICE), "Who's that tripping over my bridge?" With his heart in his throat, the scared goat replied (MEDIUM VOICE), "It is only I, the second Billy Goat. I must cross the bridge so that I can eat the grass on the other side." The troll (SCARY FACE) cackled (LOUD VOICE), "Now I am going to gobble you up!" But as the troll (SCARY FACE) began to appear over the side of the bridge, the Billy Goat cried out (MEDIUM VOICE), "Oh, no, you don't want to eat me! I am not nearly big enough to eat. Wait for my brother. He is coming after me, and he is much bigger than I am."

Fables and Folktales © Prufrock Press Inc.   95

Permission is granted to photocopy or reproduce this page for single classroom use only.

The troll (SCARY FACE) thought about this and declared (LOUD VOICE), "Very well, then, be off with you!" The middle Billy Goat Gruff (GRRUUFF) ran swiftly across the bridge to join his littlest brother on the hillside.

Seeing his brothers across the valley happily eating the new grass, the oldest Billy Goat Gruff (GRRUUFF) decided that he was not afraid of the terrible troll. He stomped down the hill until he came to the bridge. As he crossed the bridge—"trip, trap, trip, trap, trip, trap" (DRUM BEATS), the horrible troll (SCARY FACE) roared to life under the bridge, saying (LOUD VOICE), "Who's that tripping over my bridge?" With his equally frightening voice, the largest Billy Goat Gruff (GRRUUFF) replied (LOUD VOICE), "It is only I, the largest Billy Goat. I must cross the bridge so that I can eat the grass on the other side." The troll cackled (LOUD VOICE), "Now I am going to gobble you up!" The Billy Goat Gruff (GRRUUFF) replied (LOUD VOICE), "Well, come along! I've got two spears, and I'll poke your eyeballs out at your ears; I've got two curling stones, and I'll crush you to bits, body and bones." The angry troll (SCARY FACE) climbed up on the bridge to do battle with the insolent Billy Goat, but the creature's horns stabbed him and his hooves crushed him, and the largest Billy Goat Gruff (GRRUUFF) threw the troll back into the water. The troll (SCARY FACE) floated off down the river and was never heard from again. As for the largest Billy Goat Gruff (GRRUUFF), he joined his brothers on the green hillside, where they ate grass and grew fat for the winter.

Word Stress: Gruff (GRRUUFF).

Facial Expression: Troll (SCARY FACE).

Repeated refrain: When each of the first two Billy Goats Gruff protests, the refrain should be said at different pitches (softly for the first brother, and more loudly for the middle brother), but the rhythm and cadence should be the same to emphasize the repeat.

Sound Effect: Drum beats.

Changing Pitch and/or Volume: Vary pitch and volume depending on the speaker (LOUD, HIGH, MEDIUM VOICE).

Lesson 9

Concepts
- Breaking tasks into steps
- Accepting and responding to constructive criticism

Materials
- Step chart (p. 100)
- Storytelling festival schedule (p. 101)

Student Objective
Students make preparations for the storytelling festival.

Introduction
The teacher reviews the project timeframe and due date benchmarks with students.

Recognition
Students report on their progress to date, either individually or one by one in class. Students then sign up for performance times on the storytelling festival schedule.

Application
Students complete the step chart.
1. Students should ensure that they have completed all of the tasks required of them up to this point.
2. Students should complete the self-check, focusing on areas where they could improve.

3. Students generate a to-do list of steps that remain, which they will focus on later in the lesson.

Problem Solving

Students should work in pairs (mini-workshops) in order to further understand what they need to do in order to finalize their projects.

1. Students should give their presentations to partners and have their partners complete the partner check section on the step chart.
2. After the self-check and the partner check have been completed, students should work on revising their work orally and rehearsing their performances. They may do this individually or with their same partners.

Grade-Level Expectations

The student will:

- Demonstrate an initial understanding of the elements of literary texts by identifying or describing character(s), setting, problem/solution, and plot, as appropriate to the text, and by identifying any significant changes in character or setting over time.
- Analyze and interpret the elements of literary texts, citing evidence where appropriate, by describing characters' traits, motivations, and interactions and citing thoughts, words, and actions that reveal characters' personalities and changes over time.
- Demonstrate an initial understanding of the elements of literary texts by identifying the characteristics of a variety of types/genres of literary texts (e.g., poetry, plays, fairytales, fantasy, fables, realistic fiction, folktales, historical fiction, mysteries, science fiction, myths, legends).
- Analyze and interpret the elements of literary texts, citing evidence where appropriate, by making inferences about cause/effect, external conflicts (e.g., person vs. person, person vs. nature/society/fate), and the relationships among elements within text (e.g., how the historical era influences the characters' actions or thinking).

Additional Notes

- In planning the storytelling festival, you might consider whether you want to decorate the room and/or provide food and beverages at the festival. You will also want to evaluate the classroom to see whether it would be helpful to rearrange furniture or make other adjustments.
- The more you emphasize the importance of the event, the more seriously your students will take their performances; we have found that when we made a big deal out of the storytelling festival, students really rose to the occasion. You might consider inviting parents and other classes.

- However, if you do decide to invite outsiders, we recommend doing a class-only performance of the festival in advance. This way, students get some practice, you can work out the kinks, and you can complete a rubric for each student that is not scored during the bigger event, taking off some of the pressure.
- In terms of scheduling the festival, it is reasonable to expect to schedule 10–12 stories for a 50-minute class period. Most classes will need at least 2 days for this culminating activity.

Name:_____   Date: _____

Step Chart

STEP	DETAIL	DATE DUE	COMPLETED
1	Complete the planning page.		
2	Meet with the teacher and discuss your plan.		
3	Get teacher approval of your story plan.		
4	Complete a rough draft of your story.		
		SELF-CHECK	PARTNER CHECK
5	My purpose or theme is clear.		
6	My story includes a beginning, a middle, and an end that flow from one to another.		
7	I include symbolism in my story.		
8	I use a range of volume and tone to bring my story to life as I tell my story.		
9	I include descriptive and powerful words.		
10	I have rehearsed my story and can tell it without my notes.		

TO-DO LIST

1.

2.

3.

4.

5.

6.

7.

8.

9.

10.

Fables and Folktales © Prufrock Press Inc.

Schedule

Storytelling Festival Schedule

	Date	Time	Name	Title
1				
2				
3				
4				
5				
6				
7				
8				
9				
10				
11				
12				

Lesson 10

Concepts

- Accepting constructive criticism
- Theme and moral of a story

Materials

- 3" x 5" notecards or half sheets of paper for student responses
- Self-Reflection sheet (p. 104)

Student Objective

Students tell their original stories to the class. Student audience members provide written feedback for their peers.

Introduction

The teacher hands out 3" x 5" cards to all students and instructs them to fill in the performing student's name, as well as their own name. The teacher reviews the concepts of constructive criticism, positive feedback, and a story's theme or message. The teacher reviews the daily schedule of performers.

Recognition

Students give verbal examples of acceptable comments and possible themes and morals.

Application

Students tell their stories and give and receive feedback.

1. Students do not fill out a card for the student who immediately precedes them. This provides students with a few minutes to compose themselves for their story presentations.

2. Classmates fill out a card with at least one piece of constructive criticism, one positive comment, and what they believe to be the theme of the story.
3. At the end of each class, students sort the cards into piles for each performing student.

Problem Solving

Students reflect on their experiences in the unit.
1. Students consider the feedback they received.
2. Students write reflections, focusing both on what they did well and what they will work on in the future when telling stories and presenting before an audience.

Grade-Level Expectations

The student will:
- Tell stories, giving information using details and providing a coherent conclusion.
- Provide effective and appropriate feedback.
- Use a variety of strategies to engage the audience.

Additional Notes

- The peer cards are very important for both the presenter (you will find that presenters take their feedback very seriously) and the audience.
- Think through how the cards will be sorted—if you have to sort 300 cards (30 students and 10 presenters) after each class, you will be overwhelmed! Have each student sort his or her cards and put them in a specific spot for each presenter.
- Each time we teach this unit, we are surprised by at least one student who we did not expect to "wow" the audience. One would think that after helping students with editing and seeing them practice, there would be no surprises, but there always are! The first time we taught this unit, one student refused to write down anything. Throughout the entire process, he was very opposed to the idea of the storytelling workshop—the description "reluctant writer" was an understatement. Imagine our surprise when he got up to tell his story and kept the class completely spellbound for 10 minutes with an incredible story! We hope you have some similar pleasant surprises while teaching this unit.

Name: _____   Date: _____

Self-Reflection

After reviewing your peer comment cards, please answer the following questions:

1. My strengths as a storyteller are:

   _____

   _____

   _____

2. The biggest challenge for me as a storyteller is:

   _____

   _____

   _____

3. The next time I write or tell a story, I want to focus more on:

   _____

   _____

   _____

4. The best part about the Storytelling Festival was:

   _____

   _____

   _____

Appendix
Student Context Rubric

The Student Context Rubric (SCR) is intended for use by the classroom teacher as a tool to help in the identification of students of masked potential. This term, *masked potential*, refers to students who are gifted, but are frequently not identified because their behaviors are not displayed to best advantage by traditional methods. The SCR was designed to be used with this series of units and the authentic performance assessments that accompany them. Although you may choose to run the units without using the SCR, you may find the rubric helpful for keeping records of student behaviors.

The units serve as platforms for the display of student behaviors, while the SCR is an instrument that teachers can use to record those behaviors when making observations. The rubric requires the observer to record the frequency of gifted behaviors, but there is also the option to note that the student demonstrates the behavior with particular intensity. In this way, the rubric is subjective and requires careful observation and consideration.

It is recommended that an SCR be completed for each student prior to the application of a unit, and once again upon completion of the unit. In this way, teachers will be reminded of behaviors to look for during the unit—particularly those behaviors that we call *loophole behaviors*, which may indicate giftedness but are often misinterpreted or overlooked. (For instance, a student's verbal ability can be missed if he or she uses it to spin wild lies about having neglected to complete an assignment.) Therefore, the SCR allows teachers to be aware of—and to document—high-ability behavior even if it is masked or used in nontraditional ways. The mechanism also provides a method for tracking changes in teachers' perceptions of their students, not only while students are working on the Interactive Discovery-Based Units for High-Ability Learners, but also while they are engaged in traditional classroom activities.

In observing student behaviors, you might consider some of the following questions after completing a lesson:

- Was there anyone or anything that surprised you today?
- Did a particular student jump out at you today?
- Did someone come up with a unique or unusual idea today?
- Was there a moment in class today when you saw a lightbulb go on? Did it involve an individual, a small group, or the class as a whole?
- In reviewing written responses after a class discussion, were you surprised by anyone (either because he or she was quiet during the discussion but had good written ideas, or because he or she was passionate in the discussion but did not write with the same passion)?
- Did any interpersonal issues affect the classroom today? If so, how were these issues resolved?
- Did the lesson go as planned today? Were there any detours?
- Is there a student whom you find yourself thinking or worrying about outside of school?
- Are there students in your classroom who seem to be on a rollercoaster of learning—"on" one day, but "off" the next?
- Are your students different outside of the classroom? In what ways are they different?
- Are there students who refuse to engage with the project?
- During a class performance, did the leadership of a group change when students got in front of their peers?
- Did your students generate new ideas today?
- What was the energy like in your class today? Did you provide the energy, or did the students?
- How long did it take the students to engage today?

Ideally, multiple observers complete the SCR for each student. If a gifted and talented specialist is available, we recommend that he or she assist. By checking off the appropriate marks to describe student behaviors, and by completing the scoring chart, participants generate quantifiable data that can be used in advocating for students who would benefit from scaffolded services. **In terms of students' scores on the SCR, we do not provide concrete cutoffs or point requirements regarding which students should be recommended for special services.** Rather, the SCR is intended to flag students for scaffolded services and to enable them to reach their potential. It also provides a way to monitor and record students' behaviors.

What follows is an explanation of the categories and items included on the SCR, along with some examples of how the specified student behaviors might be evidenced in your classroom.

Engagement

1. **Student arrives in class with new ideas to bring to the project that he or she has thought of outside of class.** New ideas may manifest themselves as ideas about how to approach a problem, about new research information found on the Internet or elsewhere outside of class, about something in the news or in the paper that is relevant to the subject, or about a connection between the subject and an observed behavior.

2. **Student shares ideas with a small group of peers, but may fade into the background in front of a larger group.** The student may rise to be a leader when the small group is working on a project, but if asked to get up in front of the class, then that student fades into the background and lets others do the talking.

3. **Student engagement results in a marked increase in the quality of his or her performance.** This is particularly evident in a student who does not normally engage in class at all. During the unit, the student suddenly becomes engaged and produces something amazing.

4. **Student eagerly interacts with appropriate questions, but may be reluctant to put things down on paper.** This is an example of a loophole behavior, or one that causes a student to be overlooked when teachers and specialists are identifying giftedness. It is particularly evident in students who live in largely "oral" worlds, which is to say that they communicate best verbally and are often frustrated by written methods, or in those who have writing disabilities.

Creativity

1. **Student intuitively makes "leaps" in his or her thinking.** Occasionally, you will be explaining something, and a lightbulb will go on for a student, causing him or her to take the concept far beyond the content being covered. Although there are students who do this with regularity, it is more often an intensity behavior, meaning that when it occurs, the student is very intense in his or her thinking, creativity, reasoning, and so on. This can be tricky to identify, because often, the student is unable to explain his or her thinking, and the teacher realizes only later that a leap in understanding was achieved.

2. **Student makes up new rules, words, or protocols to express his or her own ideas.** This can take various forms, one of which is a student's taking two words and literally combining them to try to express what he or she is thinking about. Other times, a student will want to change the rules to make his or her idea possible.

3. **Student thinks on his or her feet in response to a project challenge, to make excuses, or to extend his or her work.** This is another loophole

behavior, because it often occurs when a student is being defensive or even misbehaving, making a teacher less likely to interpret it as evidence of giftedness. It is sometimes on display during classroom debates and discussions.

4. **Student uses pictures or other inventive means to illustrate his or her ideas.** Given the choice, this student would rather draw an idea than put it into words. This could take the shape of the student creating a character web or a design idea. The student might also act out an idea or use objects to demonstrate understanding.

Synthesis

1. **Student goes above and beyond directions to expand ideas.** It is wonderful to behold this behavior in students, particularly when displayed by those students who are rarely engaged. A student may be excited about a given idea and keep generating increasingly creative or complex material to expand upon that idea. For instance, we had a student who, during the mock trial unit, became intrigued by forensic evidence and decided to generate and interpret evidence to bolster his team's case.

2. **Student has strong opinions on projects, but may struggle to accept directions that contradict his or her opinions.** This student may understand directions, but be unwilling to yield to an idea that conflicts with his or her own idea. This behavior, rather than indicating a lack of understanding, is typical of students with strong ideas.

3. **Student is comfortable processing new ideas.** This behavior is evident in students who take new ideas and quickly extend them or ask insightful questions.

4. **Student blends new and old ideas.** This behavior has to do with processing a new idea, retrieving an older idea, and relating the two to one another. For instance, a student who learns about using string to measure distance might remember making a treasure map and extrapolate that a string would have been useful for taking into account curves and winding paths.

Interpersonal Ability

1. **Student is an academic leader who, when engaged, increases his or her levels of investment and enthusiasm in the group.** This is a student who has so much enthusiasm for learning that he or she makes the project engaging for the whole group, fostering an attitude of motivation or optimism.

2. **Student is a social leader in the classroom, but may not be an academic leader.** To observe this type of behavior, you may have to be vigilant, for some students are disengaged in the classroom but come alive as soon as they cross the threshold into the hallway, where they can socialize with their

peers. Often, this student is able to get the rest of the group to do whatever he or she wants (and does not necessarily use this talent for good).

3. **Student works through group conflict to enable the group to complete its work.** When the group has a conflict, this is the student who solves the problem or addresses the issue so that the group can get back to work. This is an interpersonal measure, and thus, it does not describe a student who simply elects to do all of the work rather than confronting his or her peers about sharing the load.

4. **Student is a Tom Sawyer in classroom situations, using his or her charm to get others to do the work.** There is an important distinction to watch out for when identifying this type of behavior: You must be sure that the student is *not* a bully, coercing others to do his or her work. Instead, this student actually makes other students *want* to lend a helping hand. For instance, a twice-exceptional student who is highly talented but struggles with reading might develop charm in order to get other students to transpose his verbally expressed ideas into writing.

Verbal Communication

1. **Participation in brainstorming sessions (e.g., group work) increases student's productivity.** When this type of student is given the opportunity to verbally process with peers, he or she is often able to come up with the answer. For instance, if asked outright for an answer, this student may shrug, but if given a minute to consult with a neighbor, then the student usually is able and willing to offer the correct answer.

2. **Student constructively disagrees with peers and/or the teacher by clearly sharing his or her thoughts.** This student can defend his or her point of view with examples and reasoning—not just in a formal debate, but also in general classroom situations. He or she has learned to channel thoughts into constructive disagreement, rather than flying off the handle merely to win an argument.

3. **Student verbally expresses his or her academic and/or social needs.** This student can speak up when confused or experiencing personality clashes within a group. This student knows when to ask for help and can clearly articulate what help is needed.

4. **Student uses strong word choice and a variety of tones to bring expression to his or her verbal communication.** This student is an engaging speaker and speaks loudly and clearly enough for everybody to hear. A wide vocabulary is also indicative that this student's verbal capability is exceptional.

Student: _____

Date: _____

Fill out the rubric according to what you have observed about each student's behaviors. Then, for each area, record the number of items you marked "Not observed," "Sometimes," and "Often." Multiply these tallies by the corresponding point values (0, 1, and 2) to get the totals for each area. There is an option to check for high intensity so you can better keep track of students' behaviors.

STUDENT CONTEXT RUBRIC

ENGAGEMENT

1. Student arrives in class with new ideas to bring to the project that he or she has thought of outside of class.
   NOT OBSERVED   SOMETIMES   OFTEN   HIGH INTENSITY

2. Student shares ideas with a small group of peers, but may fade into the background in front of a larger group.
   NOT OBSERVED   SOMETIMES   OFTEN   HIGH INTENSITY

3. Student engagement results in a marked increase in the quality of his or her performance.
   NOT OBSERVED   SOMETIMES   OFTEN   HIGH INTENSITY

4. Student eagerly interacts with appropriate questions, but may be reluctant to put things down on paper.
   NOT OBSERVED   SOMETIMES   OFTEN   HIGH INTENSITY

CREATIVITY

1. Student intuitively makes "leaps" in his or her thinking.
   NOT OBSERVED   SOMETIMES   OFTEN   HIGH INTENSITY

2. Student makes up new rules, words, or protocols to express his or her own ideas.
   NOT OBSERVED   SOMETIMES   OFTEN   HIGH INTENSITY

3. Student thinks on his or her feet in response to a project challenge, to make excuses, or to extend his or her work.
   NOT OBSERVED   SOMETIMES   OFTEN   HIGH INTENSITY

4. Student uses pictures or other inventive means to illustrate his or her ideas.
   NOT OBSERVED   SOMETIMES   OFTEN   HIGH INTENSITY

SYNTHESIS

1. Student goes above and beyond directions to expand ideas.
   NOT OBSERVED   SOMETIMES   OFTEN   HIGH INTENSITY

2. Student has strong opinions on projects, but may struggle to accept directions that contradict his or her opinions.
   NOT OBSERVED   SOMETIMES   OFTEN   HIGH INTENSITY

3. Student is comfortable processing new ideas.
   NOT OBSERVED   SOMETIMES   OFTEN   HIGH INTENSITY

4. Student blends new ideas and old ideas.
   NOT OBSERVED   SOMETIMES   OFTEN   HIGH INTENSITY

INTERPERSONAL ABILITY

1. Student is an academic leader who, when engaged, increases his or her levels of investment and enthusiasm in the group.
   NOT OBSERVED   SOMETIMES   OFTEN   HIGH INTENSITY

2. Student is a social leader in the classroom, but may not be an academic leader.
   NOT OBSERVED   SOMETIMES   OFTEN   HIGH INTENSITY

3. Student works through group conflict to enable the group to complete its work.
   NOT OBSERVED   SOMETIMES   OFTEN   HIGH INTENSITY

4. Student is a Tom Sawyer in classroom situations, using his or her charm to get others to do the work.
   NOT OBSERVED   SOMETIMES   OFTEN   HIGH INTENSITY

VERBAL COMMUNICATION

1. Participation in brainstorming sessions (e.g., group work) increases student's productivity.
   NOT OBSERVED   SOMETIMES   OFTEN   HIGH INTENSITY

2. Student constructively disagrees with peers and/or the teacher by clearly sharing his or her thoughts.
   NOT OBSERVED   SOMETIMES   OFTEN   HIGH INTENSITY

3. Student verbally expresses his or her academic and/or social needs.
   NOT OBSERVED   SOMETIMES   OFTEN   HIGH INTENSITY

4. Student uses strong word choice and a variety of tones to bring expression to his or her verbal communication.
   NOT OBSERVED   SOMETIMES   OFTEN   HIGH INTENSITY

AREA	NOT 0	SOME 1	OFTEN 2	HIGH	TOTAL
ENGAGEMENT					
CREATIVITY					
SYNTHESIS					
INTERPERSONAL ABILITY					
VERBAL COMMUNICATION					
ADD TOTALS					

Developed by Cote & Blauvelt under the auspices of the Further Steps Forward Project, a Jacob Javits grant program, #S206A050086.

Fables and Folktales © Prufrock Press Inc.

About the Authors

Darcy O. Blauvelt has been teaching in a variety of facilities for more than 12 years. Her educational journey has included public schools, private schools, nursery schools, and a professional theatre for children ages 3–18. Blauvelt holds educational certification in Theatre K–12, Early Childhood Education, and English Education 5–12. She holds a B.A. in theatre from Chatham College, Pittsburgh, PA, and has done graduate work at Lesley University in Massachusetts in creative arts in learning, as well as at Millersville University in Pennsylvania in psychology.

In 2005, she joined the Nashua School District as a gifted and talented resource specialist. Subsequently, she served full time as the program coordinator for the Further Steps Forward Project, a Javits Grant program, from 2005–2009. Blauvelt returned to the classroom in the fall of 2009 and currently teaches seventh-grade English in Nashua, NH. Blauvelt lives in Manchester, NH with her husband, two dogs, five cats, and the occasional son!

Richard G. Cote, M.B.A., is a career educator. He has dedicated 41 years to being a classroom teacher (mathematics, physics), a community college adjunct instructor (economics), a gifted and talented resource specialist, and the director of the Further Steps Forward Project, a Javits Grant program.

His development of the MESH (mathematics, English, science, and history) program has led him to several audiences. He has presented at various national conventions, civic/community groups, district school boards, teacher organizations, community colleges, and universities, and has served as a consultant to educators throughout the country. Cote helped develop the teacher certification examination for physics at the Institute for Educational Testing and Research at the University of South Florida. He completed the Florida Council on Educational Management Program in Educational Leadership, and he is the recipient of numerous awards, including a certificate of merit on economics education from the University of South Florida, a grant from the Florida Council on Economics Education, a Florida Compact award, and prestigious NAGC Curriculum Studies awards for the development of *Mathematics in the Marketplace, Order in the Court, Ecopolis,* and *What's Your Opinion?*

Now retired from the workplace, Cote continues to share his energy, creativity, and expertise with educators through the Interactive Discovery-Based Units for High-Ability Learners.